# YOUNG PERSON'S
# Career
# SKILLS
# HANDBOOK

by the EDITORS at JIST

**Also in JIST's Young Person's Handbook Series™**

*Young Person's Occupational Outlook Handbook*

*Young Person's Character Education Handbook*

**JIST**
*Works*
America's Career Publisher

D0723072

## Young Person's Career Skills Handbook

© 2006 by JIST Publishing, Inc.

Published by JIST Works, an imprint of JIST Publishing, Inc.
8902 Otis Avenue
Indianapolis, IN 46216-1033
Phone: 1-800-648-JIST          Fax: 1-800-JIST-FAX
E-mail: info@jist.com          Web site: www.jist.com

> **Note to educators.** *Young Person's Career Skills Handbook* is part of JIST's Young Person's Handbook Series. Related resources include career-related videos, workbooks, assessments, and much more. Call 1-800-648-JIST or visit www.jist.com for more information.
>
> Quantity discounts are available for JIST products. Have future editions of JIST books delivered to you through our convenient standing order program. Please call 1-800-648-JIST or visit www.jist.com for a free catalog and more information.
>
> Visit www.jist.com for information on JIST; book excerpts; and ordering information on our many products. For free information on 14,000 job titles, visit www.careeroink.com.

Acquisitions Editor: Susan Pines
Writer: Nancy Stevenson
Development Editor: Heather Stith
Cover Designer and Illustrator: Chris Sabatino
Interior Illustrator: George McKeon
Interior Designer: Nick Anderson
Interior Layout: Trudy Coler
Proofreaders: Jeanne Clark, Paula Lowell and Linda Quigley

Printed in the United States of America

11  10  09  08  07  06          9  8  7  6  5  4  3  2  1

Library of Congress Cataloging-in-Publication Data
Young person's career skills handbook / by the editors at JIST.
     p. cm. -- (JIST's young person's handbook series)
  Includes index.
  ISBN-13: 978-1-59357-243-3 (alk. paper)
  ISBN-10: 1-59357-243-3 (alk. paper)
  1. Vocational qualifications--Juvenile literature. 2. Vocational guidance--Juvenile literature. I. JIST Works, Inc. II. Series.
  HF5381.6.Y68 2006
  331.702--dc22
                                        2006008663

ISBN-13: 1-978-1-59357-243-3
ISBN-10: 1-59357-243-3

# About This Book

Skills are things that you do well. Everyone—including you—has many skills! Your skills affect your whole life, including how well you do in school, what interests you, how you spend your free time, and what career you choose. Skills are the building blocks for a happy and successful life.

Career skills are the abilities that employers want from their workers on the job. Did you know that many of the skills you are learning in school will someday help you in your career? Because career skills build on each other, understanding and learning them now will help you get better and better at them.

This handbook opens your eyes to the career skills that will help you succeed at any job. The book includes many interesting examples, stories, checklists, activities, and other features to help you explore and begin developing career skills.

The introduction gives you more information on how to use the book. We hope the *Young Person's Career Skills Handbook* helps you learn more about career skills.

# TABLE OF CONTENTS

# INTRODUCTION

This book is designed to help you understand and explore a wide variety of career skills. This is important because the skills you bring to your career determine how successful you will be.

It is important that you begin to develop career skills now, so that you will be prepared to find and hold a good job. Always remember: Success is measured not only by the salary you receive, but by the satisfaction you get from using your skills and doing your job well.

This book is divided into two parts: "Foundation Skills" and "Workplace Skills." Foundation skills are basic skills that everybody needs to succeed and that you should be learning now, such as reading, writing, creative thinking, and honesty. Workplace skills are necessary in many jobs, and you can develop many of these skills today in school and later on the job. For example, working on a team, managing your time, and communicating information are needed in almost every occupation.

Note that many of these skills work in combination. For example, the foundation skill of reasoning may help you when interpreting information on the job.

The key goal is to learn about the skills that will help you enter and excel in any career you choose. This book helps you get started.

## Background on the Career Skills

This book gives descriptions of 36 important career skills, sometimes called the "SCANS skills" or just "SCANS." SCANS stands for Secretary's Commission on Achieving Necessary Skills. The commission was organized by the U.S. Secretary of Labor. Its purpose was to research which skills employers wanted most in their workers and to investigate whether young people were learning these skills.

Their report listed the 36 career skills described fully in this book. The report said that schools need to teach the skills to students to prepare them for future success. So get a head start on your career skills!

## How to Use This Book

You can use this book in many ways. For example, you can

- Read it from beginning to end if you want to learn about all the skills.
- Study the skills in any order.
- Read the skills that interest you the most or that you want to develop.
- Refer to the book when you are researching careers that fit your skills and interests.

If you are using this book in a class, your teacher may assign the material for reading, group discussion, extra credit, homework, or even role-playing.

## Information Provided for Each Skill

Each skill in this book follows the same format, so the information is easy to use. Each skill "chapter" includes these sections:

- *Careers That Use This Skill.* A list of careers that focus on this skill.
- *Why Employers Want This Skill.* An explanation of why this skill is important to employers and businesses for success and profit.
- *This Skill on the Job.* A first-person case study of a situation or job that uses the skill.

- *Build Your Skills.* Suggestions of courses to take today and in the future that will help you develop this skill, plus activities and projects you can do now to build the skill.

- *Try It Yourself.* A job situation where the skill is needed, together with steps you might take to put the skill in action.

- *Performance Review.* Your self-rating for the skill and a checklist for self-improvement.

- *Words at Work.* Vocabulary words related to the skill.

Appendixes describe other resources and core subjects for learning more about career skills. Remember that your teachers, counselor, and family can also help you learn about and develop your career skills.

# PART I

## Foundation Skills

The skills explained in Part I are important in school, in careers, and in life. They are called foundation skills because everything else you learn builds on them. What do you think would happen to a house without a good foundation? With strong foundation skills, you will be more successful at school and in your future.

As you read Part I, imagine that each skill is part of a foundation. If you leave out some skills, what happens to your foundation?

### Basic Skills

You are learning basic skills in school and using them everyday. Which skills do you like to use best? Which skills are you good at already? Why do you think these skills are called basic skills?

*Career Skill 1:* Reading

*Career Skill 2:* Writing

*Career Skill 3:* Working with Numbers

*Career Skill 4:* Listening

*Career Skill 5:* Speaking

## Thinking Skills

Clear thinking skills open your world to learning and creativity, help you make good choices, and help you solve problems. Your future boss will value your ability to think, but you need to start practicing that skill now. How do these skills strengthen your foundation?

*Career Skill 6:* Thinking Creatively

*Career Skill 7:* Making Decisions

*Career Skill 8:* Solving Problems

*Career Skill 9:* Visualizing

*Career Skill 10:* Knowing How to Learn

*Career Skill 11:* Reasoning

## Personal Qualities

These skills are important for getting along with others, doing a good job without someone reminding you, and feeling positive. How are you developing and using these skills already? What happens to your foundation if you are not responsible? Why is honesty important now and in your future? How do you think these personal qualities build on each other?

*Career Skill 12:* Being Responsible

*Career Skill 13:* Having Self-Esteem

*Career Skill 14:* Being Sociable

*Career Skill 15:* Managing Yourself

*Career Skill 16:* Being Honest

# READING

**P**eople often share information through written words. Today, you may read those words on a computer screen, on a cell phone display, in a book, or in a printed or handwritten note. But beyond reading and understanding what you read, you often have to make choices about which information is most useful or accurate. Employers consider the ability to identify relevant and accurate information to be important in almost any job.

The skill of reading includes the ability to

- Identify relevant facts
- Locate information
- Find meanings of words
- Judge accuracy of information
- Use a computer to find information

## Careers That Use This Skill

**A**ny worker will do better by having this skill, but these careers are strongly focused on being able to read:

- Librarians
- Researchers
- Writers
- Trainers and teachers
- Journalists
- Editors

- Lawyers
- Telemarketers
- Proofreaders
- File Clerks
- Speech-language pathologists

# Why Employers Want This Skill

**M**any jobs involve gathering information and reading about your customers and competitors. You can then use that information to make decisions about your business. Other jobs require that you read manuals or online instructions to perform a task.

When employers hire a person for a job, they often test that person's ability to read and understand what is read. There's a lot of information out there these days, on the Internet, on television—everywhere! Employees who can use all these sources and come up with the best information are usually more successful.

Workers on the shop floor reading instructions for operating a machine, cooks reading recipes, and network technicians reading how to install software all rely on information to do their work. Good reading skills are what help you find and understand that information.

> **"** *Reading is a basic tool in the living of a good life.* **"**
> —Joseph Addison, writer

# Reading on the Job

Name: Marietta Duprix

Job: Community center volunteer

*I love to play the piano, but I can't afford one of my own. I worked out a deal with the people at the community center to help out every Saturday for a few hours in exchange for the use of their piano. Sometimes I file papers, sometimes I clean the kitchen, and sometimes I sign up people for various programs.*

*You might not think this type of work requires many reading skills, but it does. When I file papers, I have to skim each document to figure out what it's about to figure out what folder I should put it in. I have to read the directions and safety warnings written on cleaning products to make sure I'm using them correctly when I clean the kitchen. When I sign up people for programs, I have to look up fees and program numbers in the catalog. Sometimes I help people to fill out the program registration forms by reading the forms and explaining what they should write.*

> **❝** Nature and books belong to the eyes that see them. **❞**
>
> —Ralph Waldo Emerson, writer

# Build Your Skills

**R**eading is taught at every school, but you can become a more effective reader through your education and activities.

### Education

- Take courses in English, writing, and literature.
- For extra credit, write book reports about books you have read.
- If you have difficulty understanding what you read, ask your English teacher for extra help or find a reading tutor.

### Activities

- Join reading-oriented groups such as book reading clubs or library groups.
- Read a new book every week.
- Read your newspaper every day and ask questions of others if you don't understand something you read.
- Gather friends together to read stories or plays out loud to each other. Discuss the meanings of the works afterward.
- Read articles in magazines or online. Outline the key points in the article to get better at identifying relevant facts.
- Go to the library and learn how to find information you need for projects or hobbies.
- Practice browsing for information on the Internet.

# Try It Yourself

Imagine that you're helping out your dad, who owns a toy store, before the holiday rush. Your dad has asked you to find a new supplier for train sets because the old supplier is going out of business. Follow these steps to put your reading skills to work:

1. Create a list of four companies that make train sets. To find this information, you could search the Internet or look in your local phone book.

2. Get brochures from each company or print out information about the companies from the Internet. You can call each company on the phone or order catalogs online.

3. Create a table with the following headings: Company, Location, Price Range, Shipping Charges, and Products. Using the information you have about each company, fill in a row in the table for each. Try to find similar products to compare prices. In the Product column, list the number of product lines each company carries. In the Shipping column, note whether they have free shipping or offer rush shipping.

4. Draw conclusions. Using the information you have gathered with your reading, decide which company you would recommend to your dad.

How useful was being able to read in completing this task? When you think about it, many of the projects or assignments you do every day involve reading. Once you read information, you often have to use it to make a decision, build something, find your way to a location, and more. Just about every job in the world involves the skill of reading.

# Performance Review

**W**hat rating would an employer give you on your reading skills?

- Needs Improvement
- Average
- Above Average
- Outstanding

Use the methods in the following checklist to become an outstanding reader.

---

## READING CHECKLIST

- ◯ Use computers, books, and other sources to locate information.
- ◯ Increase your vocabulary by reading a variety of materials. Look up words you don't understand in the dictionary.
- ◯ When you read a news story, short story, or article, identify the most important information.
- ◯ Evaluate the information you read. Is it accurate and true?

---

# Words at Work

**T**hese words relate to understanding what you read. How many can you define?

- Relevant
- Accuracy
- Interpret
- Specifications
- Data
- Infer
- Plausibility
- Vocabulary

# WRITING

**J**ust about every civilization has had a written language. Writing provides a way to record information so that others can read it. Writing effectively involves making sure the facts are correct, being persuasive, organizing information well, and checking mechanics such as spelling and grammar. The writing process often involves drafting a document, revising it, proofreading it, and finalizing it.

The skill of writing includes the ability to

- Communicate thoughts and information in writing
- Record information completely and accurately
- Use appropriate language, style, organization, and format
- Include supporting documentation
- Check, edit, and revise written material for correctness

## Careers That Use This Skill

**A**ny worker will do better by having this skill, but these careers are strongly focused on being able to write:

- Journalists
- Technical writers
- Advertising copywriters
- Editors
- Administrative assistants
- Paralegals
- Publicists

# Why Employers Want This Skill

**P**eople who can write effectively often find that they get ahead on the job. Their words have an impact beyond the few people they can speak with everyday. For example, a well-written report or memo might go to hundreds of people who will recognize the writer's achievement. A poorly written document can also reflect on a writer, holding him or her back in the workplace.

Some jobs are directly related to writing. For example, if you are a copywriter at an advertising agency writing ads or a screenwriter writing movie scripts, you were hired to write full time. Other jobs are not directly related to writing, but still use writing to communicate information or to persuade people. Accountants, lawyers, and people who have to promote their own small businesses have to be able to write well, for example.

When a company interviews you for a job, you will often be tested on your ability to write and organize information. If you have a good vocabulary, can organize your thoughts, and have mastered grammar and spelling, you will probably do well.

Though a few jobs do not require writing, if you want to move up in the workplace over the years, you can only benefit from strong writing skills. Whether your work involves filling out forms clearly or writing lengthy reports, you will find that writing skills will come in handy over time.

# Writing on the Job

Name: Chris Perez

Job: Part-time worker in his father's antiques store

*Last weekend I helped my dad catalog the inventory in the store. Dad asked me to write a brief description of each item in the Victorian section of the store. I made sure each description was complete by including information about the size, shape, and color of each item. I've worked in the store for a while so I knew exactly what to call each item so that it would be clear to Dad what it was. I grouped the objects by type, such as figurines or furniture, so that my dad and the other people who work in the store could find the information they needed more quickly.*

*Before I gave my dad the list, I looked it over to make sure I hadn't misspelled anything and that all the descriptions were clear. I didn't want Dad to spend a lot of time trying to figure out what I was describing. He said I did a great job. He even paid me extra!*

> **❝**Without words, without writing, and without books there would be no history, there could be no concept of humanity. **❞**
> —**Hermann Hesse, writer**

# Build Your Skills

You learned how to write individual letters and sentences when you were younger. But what else is involved in becoming a good writer? You can develop this important skill through your education and activities.

## Education

- Take courses in English, creative writing, and journalism.
- When you are given the choice between a written and oral report for a class, write it!
- Volunteer to write for your school yearbook, newsletter, or Web site.

## Activities

- Keep a daily journal or blog of your thoughts and activities.
- Write letters to your friends or family who are far away.
- Write articles for your local newspaper or letters to the editor when you want to comment on a local issue.
- Join a writer's group and get feedback from other writers about your writing.
- Go to the library and learn how to find information you need to make your writing accurate.
- Write postings for online discussion groups in your areas of interest.

# Try It Yourself

You've been asked to write an article for the yearbook about the various clubs at your school. Follow these steps to put your writing skills to work:

1. List the key points you wish to make by creating an outline, a basic tool used for organizing information in writing.

2. Research your topic. Do interviews; review your school or school club Web sites; and look at documents the various clubs produce, such as newsletters or announcements of activities.

3. Write a first draft of the article. Try to cover all the key points, but don't worry too much at this point about things like spelling. Get the important ideas down in a logical order.

4. Review what you've written. Take a look at your draft to see whether the ideas flow, the style is clear, and the facts are accurate. Reorganize information in a logical way. At this stage, it's often helpful to have somebody else read what you've written to see whether it's clear.

5. Proofread and correct your article. It's time to revise, make corrections, and catch errors. Use your computer spell checker function to catch spelling errors. Keep a dictionary handy to make sure you've used the correct word. Don't be afraid to cut out extra words and phrases to make your writing concise and crisp.

> **❝**The skill of writing is to create a context in which other people can think. **❞**
> —Edwin Schlossberg, designer

# Performance Review

**W**hat rating would an employer give you on your writing skills?

- Needs Improvement
- Average
- Above Average
- Outstanding

Use the methods in the following checklist to become an outstanding writer.

---

## WRITING CHECKLIST

- ◯ Organize information logically in your writing.
- ◯ Improve your vocabulary so that you can choose just the right word to get your meaning across.
- ◯ Take the time to review and revise your work and check for details such as spelling and grammar.
- ◯ Focus on getting your message across in a concise, clear way.

---

# Words at Work

**T**hese words relate to writing. How many can you define?

- Description
- Documenting
- Convey
- Proofread
- Mechanics
- Grammar
- Revise
- Concise

# WORKING WITH NUMBERS

**M**athematics deals with numbers. Working with numbers involves making calculations that help people handle many situations in their lives. From the simple addition of a column of numbers to the more complex calculations that predict the likelihood of an event, people use math to help them understand and express ideas about the world.

Working with numbers includes the ability to

- Perform basic computations including whole numbers and fractions
- Estimate mathematic results without a calculator
- Organize information with tables and graphs
- Choose from a variety of mathematical techniques to deal with practical problems

## Careers That Use This Skill

**A**ny worker will do better by having this skill, but these careers are strongly focused on working with numbers:

- Mathematicians
- Scientists
- Engineers
  - Stockbrokers
  - Accountants
- Bookkeepers
- Actuaries

- Statisticians
- Architects
- Salespeople
- Computer software engineers
- Cost estimators

# Why Employers Want This Skill

**M**any jobs deal directly with mathematics. For example, accountants, engineers, investment counselors, and bank tellers use math in their work. But many more jobs require that you use mathematics to get your job done. For example, you might be a clerk at a cash register who has to calculate a refund to a customer. Or you may be a fisherman who has to calculate the price you will charge per pound for the fish you caught today.

In a business setting, mathematics is used for many things. For example, you might add up the prices of the items on an invoice, calculate the percentage of sales to customers in Asia, or create a graph showing stock market trends.

Most jobs require employees to work with numbers at some point. You may have to do simple math, such as addition, subtraction, or division. Or you may be asked to do more complex calculations such as figuring the area of a three-dimensional object. You may have to know how to set up computer software to do some calculations for you.

> **"**The true spirit of delight, the exaltation, the sense of being more than Man, which is the touchstone of the highest excellence, is to be found in mathematics as surely as in poetry.**"**
> —Bertrand Russell, philosopher and essayist

# Working with Numbers on the Job

Name: Christian McNamara

Job: Self-employed painter

*When I find people who want their house painted, one of the first things I do is give them a bid for how much the job will cost. There's a lot of different numbers involved in coming up with a final price. First I have to figure out how many hours it will take to complete the job. Last week, for example, I came up with a bid for my neighbor Mrs. Martini. She wanted her kitchen and dining room painted. I went to her house and measured the rooms to figure out how much surface I would have to cover. I also looked at how much molding and trim I would have to paint around because that takes longer to do than plain walls. Finally, I looked at the original color of the walls and the color of the paint she wanted me to use to figure out how many coats I would need to do. I used all this information to estimate how many hours it should take me to complete the work.*

*The trickiest part of coming up with a price is setting a value on my time. If I set my price too high, customers will hire a cheaper painter, and I won't have any work. If I set my price too low, I won't make enough to cover my business expenses, such as equipment costs, and earn a decent salary. I always keep track of what other painters in the area are charging. I've also worked hard to build a good reputation as a painter. My customers are often willing to pay me a little more because I do a great job!*

# Build Your Skills

You study math in school, but you can do more to gain skill in working with numbers.

**Education**

- Take courses in algebra and geometry. Algebra helps you with basic equations, and geometry helps you to measure and calculate the shapes of objects.

- Take classes to learn to use computer software that helps you calculate formulas, such as spreadsheet programs.

- Take courses in accounting to learn how to work with calculations concerning money.

**Activities**

- Keep a record of your own expenses and work up a monthly budget.

- Join a club or activity where math is involved, such as a club for people who work on electronics projects. Or serve as treasurer for a club to gain practice in managing budgets.

- Keep track of a particular stock's value on the stock market using the Internet. Create a graph showing the stock's highs and lows over a six-month period.

- Read books on mathematics and mathematical theory.

> **"Mathematics is the queen of the sciences."**
> —Carl Friedrich Gauss, mathematician and astronomer

# Try It Yourself

Your coach has asked you to create a graph showing the numbers of wins and losses your team has had over the past four years and calculate the average number of wins across that time period. Follow these steps to put your mathematical skills to work:

1. Gather the data on wins and losses. You might create a simple table with information for the year, wins, and losses to keep the data organized.

2. Enter data into a spreadsheet program. (A spreadsheet program lets you instantly generate reports and graphs from numerical data.)

3. Generate a graph. Consider the type of graph to use. Line graphs would show a horizontal line indicating the trends of wins and losses over the years. Bar graphs would show a comparison of wins to losses for each year. Spreadsheet software will help you generate different kinds of graphs instantly.

4. Calculate the average of wins for the four years by adding together all the wins for the four years and then dividing that total by four.

This example involves simple math and is made easier by the use of a spreadsheet program. If you don't have a spreadsheet program on your computer, you can still create a simple graph on paper by marking points on a scale for each number (total wins, total losses per year) and then connecting those points to create a line chart, for example.

# Performance Review

**W**hat rating would an employer give you on your ability to work with numbers?

- Needs Improvement
- Average

- Above Average
- Outstanding

Use the methods in the following checklist to earn an Outstanding rating in this skill.

---

## WORKING WITH NUMBERS CHECKLIST

- ◯ Do calculations using both whole numbers and fractions.
- ◯ Estimate results to mathematical problems.
- ◯ Use different kinds of tables, graphs, diagrams, and charts to find information.
- ◯ Write descriptions of the mathematical ideas you use to solve problems involving numbers.

---

# Words at Work

**T**hese words relate to working with numbers. How many can you define?

- Formula
- Spreadsheet
- Geometry
- Algebra

- Percentage
- Quantitative
- Estimate
- Average

# LISTENING

**C**ommunication involves two parts: somebody sends out a message, and somebody else receives and responds to it. With the spoken word, the receiving side of this partnership is called listening. Listening isn't all that easy. You have to focus on what's being said and not let your mind wander off.

The skill of listening includes the ability to

- Pay attention to and understand spoken words and other sounds
- Notice and understand the meaning of a speaker's body language and tone of voice
- Respond to the speaker appropriately

## Careers That Use This Skill

**A**ny worker will do better by having this skill, but these careers are strongly focused on being able to listen:

- Customer service representatives
- Psychiatrists
- Dispatchers
- Journalists
- Translators
- Social workers
- Food servers

- Doctors
- Bank tellers
- Computer support specialists
- Sales people
- Medical transcriptionists
- Speech-language pathologists

# Why Employers Want This Skill

**E**mployers appreciate people who can listen carefully to instructions, training, customers, other workers, and their supervisors. People who don't listen at work often get things wrong. They don't seem able to follow directions. They don't understand procedures and policies. People who listen well understand what's expected of them and make fewer mistakes.

Beyond simply hearing what's said, a good listener understands and interprets the information and responds in an appropriate way. In business, when a customer tells a salesperson that she's unhappy, that salesperson has to figure out the right way to respond to make the customer happy again. This process often involves both listening to what's being said and paying attention to other clues such as the speaker's tone of voice or body language. Body language includes actions such as fidgeting or blinking rapidly, which may indicate the speaker's state of mind.

Listening plays an important part not just in doing your job correctly, but also in getting along with others. If you listen to others at work, you can understand their point of view or feelings. If you listen carefully, you may find that a person speaking to you about work is upset or concerned about something. Good listening helps you to get those problems out in the open and solve them. If you are a manager, listening to your employees gives you the information you need to help them to get their jobs done and stay happy in their work.

> **❝**Make sure you have finished speaking before your audience has finished listening.**❞**
> —**Dorothy Sarnoff, singer**

# Listening on the Job

Name: Brett Anderson

Job: Volunteer library assistant

*I love books and want to be a librarian when I grow up, so I volunteer at the local library a few hours a week. My work usually involves reshelving the returned books. One Saturday, however, Mrs. Smith was out sick. (Mrs. Smith is the person who works at the information desk.) The head librarian, Mr. Canfield, asked all five people working that day to help people who came to the information desk. "Even me?" I asked. Mr. Canfield said, "You know this library and our systems pretty well, Brett. I don't see why you couldn't help people. If you get a tough question, just ask one of the others for help."*

*To help people at the information desk, I had to listen carefully to their questions. Sometimes I thought they were asking one thing, but when I asked them questions to make sure I understood what they were saying, I found out they were really asking something else. Once I figured out what the person was asking for, I had to decide the right way to respond. For example, somebody who was new to the library and wanted a card had to fill out a form. Somebody who wanted to replace a lost card just needed to show me identification so that I could look up the right information in the computer. A few times I had to ask one of the librarians for help because I didn't know enough to give the person the information he or she was looking for, but I was able to answer most people's questions.*

# Build Your Skills

**P**eople learn to listen when they are babies; even people with hearing challenges learn to pick up visual cues from those communicating with them. You practice listening every day, but you can do certain things to develop your listening skills.

## Education

- Take courses in speech or drama to practice speaking and listening to others speak.

- Listen closely in your classes and learn how to take good notes to help you remember important points.

- Learn another language. Listening to somebody speaking in another language can help you pay attention because your mind is actively engaged in translating each word.

## Activities

- Listen to audio books or podcasts and focus on what's being said.

- Join a debating club or book discussion group.

- If you have trouble listening, every once in a while repeat back to the speaker what you think he or she has just said in your own words.

- Study people's tone of voice and body language for clues to the meaning of what they are saying.

- Try to give the speaker an appropriate response. Nothing sends a clearer message that you're not listening than to respond to what's been said with an inappropriate comment.

# Try It Yourself

**Y**ou work two hours a week on a teen call-in show on your school's radio station. This week it's your job to answer the phone when people call in. Sometimes those people have a problem and want advice. Other times they are calling about a topic that doesn't relate to the show's topic, and you have to screen out their call. Create a listening skills checklist to help you do this job effectively. Such a list might include the following items:

1.  When answering the phone, ask for and make a note of the person's name and why he or she is calling so you know who you are talking to.

2.  Listen to the caller's tone of voice to see if he or she is upset or making a crank call.

3.  After listening to the caller, paraphrase (repeat in your own words) what you think the caller wants in order to confirm your understanding.

What other items might you include on the list? How can you use good listening skills to screen out callers who aren't appropriate for the show? Many jobs such as this one require good listening so you can make the right decision. Could you handle the call-in line on a radio show? Could you handle an emergency line at the police station? Good listening is more vital in some jobs than others, but it always comes in handy for getting the job done right.

> **❝**When we are listened to it creates us, makes us unfold and expand.**❞**
>
> —Karl Menninger, psychiatrist

# Performance Review

**W**hat rating would an employer give you on your listening skills?

- Needs Improvement
- Average
- Above Average
- Outstanding

Use the methods in the following checklist to become an outstanding listener.

---

## LISTENING CHECKLIST

- ◯ Let people finish what they are saying before responding.
- ◯ Ask questions when you don't understand what's being said.
- ◯ Avoid thinking about your own reply to what's being said and instead pay attention to the speaker.
- ◯ Notice nonverbal clues such as tone of voice or body language when somebody speaks to you. Make sure you give such clues back to the speaker to let him or her know you're listening.
- ◯ Respond in an appropriate way to what has been said.

---

# Words at Work

**T**hese words relate to listening effectively. How many can you define?

- Focus
- Response
- Body language
- Nonverbal
- Interpret
- Comprehend
- Evaluate
- Paraphrase

# SPEAKING

The spoken word can be the most persuasive and effective form of communication. That's because when you speak to an individual or group, you can use your tone of voice and body language to convey your message. In addition, when you speak to somebody in person, you can see that person's body language and expression and change what you say to fit that feedback. For example, if you explain a concept and your listener looks confused, you can explain the idea in a different way to make it clearer.

The skill of speaking includes the ability to

- Organize ideas and speak clearly and effectively
- Use a style of speaking that fits your audience
- Understand and respond to listener feedback

## Careers That Use This Skill

Any worker will do better by having this skill, but these careers are strongly focused on being able to speak:

- Politicians
- Business executives
- Television and radio announcers
- Teachers and trainers
- Lawyers
- Tour guides
- Athletic coaches
- Telemarketers
- Actors and actresses
- Receptionists

# Why Employers Want This Skill

**J**ust about any job involves speaking with people such as coworkers, customers, or suppliers. Many jobs also involve more formal speaking tasks, such as making business presentations or appearing on a television show. Some people speak or small to large groups. Others speak to only one or two people at a time.

The ability to communicate effectively through speech is important no matter what the setting. If you don't have the skills to get your ideas across to others or ask clear questions, you won't be able to do your work well. Knowing what tone and language to use when you speak also reflects on you: If you speak very informally at a formal event, your employer will feel that you are not ready to interact with others at that level.

Whether you give speeches at conventions, run a weekly staff meeting, or talk to customers on the phone or in person, the ability to speak effectively and clearly will serve you well. Good speaking skills are what help you connect with others and communicate ideas and information that help you get your work done.

> **"**It usually takes more than three weeks to prepare a good impromptu speech.**"**
> —Mark Twain, writer

# Speaking on the Job

Name: Jeff Pulaski

Job: Animal shelter volunteer

*I want to be a veterinarian someday, so I volunteer at the animal shelter one day a week. Next week is animal information week at the shelter. Each day a different school class will tour the shelter to learn about the work done there. The manager of the shelter has asked me to run one of the tours for a third grade class.*

*To prepare for the tour, I have been studying brochures and other information about the shelter and asking different workers at the shelter about their jobs. I am taking notes that I can refer to when giving the tour. I want to keep the kids interested, so I'm making sure that I learn all the facts about the things they're likely to want to know about. I'm also prepared to define any terms they may not understand. I plan to keep my talk fairly short and leave lots of time for questions. Believe me, third graders have lots of questions! I'll try to keep my answers simple because I don't want to overwhelm them. I like giving tours for younger kids because they like it when I am loud and a little silly.*

> **❝**Speak properly and in as few words as you can, but always plainly; for the end of speech is not ostentation, but to be understood.**❞**
>
> —William Penn, founder of Pennsylvania

# Build Your Skills

Though you speak every day, you have to make an investment of time and effort to become an effective speaker. You can develop this important skill through your education and activities. If you're nervous about speaking in public—and many people are—you should try to overcome that fear now so it doesn't hold you back in your career.

## Education

- Take courses in drama or speech to gain confidence in speaking.
- Engage in discussions in the classroom. Don't sit quietly when the class is talking about a topic. Jump in and say what's on your mind!
- Build a strong vocabulary by reading and looking up words that you don't understand in a dictionary.

## Activities

- Join speaking-oriented clubs such as debating or drama. An organization known as Toastmasters helps people become more comfortable with speaking in public.
- Volunteer to talk to groups about topics you know well.
- Film yourself speaking and notice any distracting mannerisms or gestures you should avoid. Record yourself and listen to your tone of voice to see whether you could improve your speech.
- Listen to speeches of others at school or on television. Do you think the President of the United States gives good speeches? Why or why not?

# Try It Yourself

**S**uppose you work part time in the office of a nonprofit group that helps homeless kids. A local civic group has asked your boss to provide a speaker who can explain the work you do. She asks you whether you would be willing to make the speech. Follow these steps to put your speaking skills to work:

1.  Try to find out something about the group you'll be talking to. If it is made up of business people, you might focus on the economics of your work. If it is made up of educators, you could focus your speech on educational programs. Search on the Internet or call the group contact and ask for some background on the membership.

2.  Find out how much time you have to speak and research the most important points you want to make in that time. Practice your speech beforehand to make sure it runs the allotted time.

3.  Organize the contents of your speech in the most logical way for the listener. Try to find a logical sequence to the information you present. For example, you could talk about your group's achievements from the time it was founded through today. This chronological order helps your listeners follow your train of thought.

4.  Build in time at the end of your speech for questions or encourage your listeners to ask questions during your talk, if you prefer.

# Performance Review

What rating would an employer give you on your speaking skills?

- Needs Improvement
- Average
- Above Average
- Outstanding

To earn an Outstanding rating, focus on the tasks in the following checklist:

---

## SPEAKING CHECKLIST

- ◯ Prepare speeches by creating outlines for the information you want to present. Make sure your information is organized so that the listener can follow along easily.

- ◯ When you participate in conversations and discussions, express your ideas clearly and confidently.

- ◯ Practice using your tone of voice, vocabulary, and nonverbal clues to help your listener understand what you're saying.

- ◯ Note how your listeners respond to what you are saying. Work on becoming comfortable responding to listener questions.

---

# Words at Work

These words relate to effective speaking. How many can you define?

- Communicate
- Gesture
- Presentation
- Convey
- Feedback
- Tone
- Clarity
- Enunciate

# THINKING CREATIVELY

Thinking is more than applying logic and organizing information. Creativity is a big part of thinking, too. Thinking creatively helps you make mental leaps from what you know to new possibilities.

People who think creatively use their imaginations to make connections that others might not make between pieces of information. In the workplace, thinking creatively helps people come up with new products, new ways of getting work done, or new ways of promoting their business.

Thinking creatively includes the ability to

- Imagine freely
- Combine information in new and interesting ways
- Connect seemingly unrelated ideas
- Change goals to reveal new possibilities

## Careers That Use This Skill

Any worker will do better by having this skill, but these careers are strongly focused on thinking creatively:

- Painters
- Inventors
- Poets
- Composers
- Graphic designers

- Directors
- Scientists
- Photographers
- Dancers
- Advertising managers

# Why Employers Want This Skill

Some jobs are thought of as creative, such as an artist, inventor, or writer, because their work is to think up new things. But almost every job can benefit from creative thinking to solve problems or find more efficient ways to get things done.

Many employers consider the ability to think creatively as one of the most prized characteristics in workers. That's because creative people are often good problem solvers. They are able to look at problems in unique ways to come up with solutions. They are the ones who come up with new ideas that help a company stand out from its competitors.

People who think creatively are never satisfied with the way things are; they think about how things could be better. They see possibilities in everything, such as tools that can be used in new ways and different ideas that can be combined to make a new idea. Creative thinking includes everything from small changes, such as coming up with a simpler way to sort the company mail, to big ideas, such as imagining a new product that makes a company millions. Creative employees don't just do work the way it's always been done, but they feel free to try new ways of doing things.

The world is constantly changing. New technologies are developed, new ideas are expressed, and new problems have to be solved. Organizations have to be able to change to stay competitive with other organizations in this country and around the world. They need employees who think creatively in order to meet the challenges of today and tomorrow.

# Thinking Creatively on the Job

Name: Kyle Williams

Job: Publicity chair for the middle school's benefit concert

*The middle school hosted a band in a concert to benefit victims of a hurricane. I was in charge of concert publicity. I had to sell 1,000 tickets in a month and a half, so it was a lot to take on. The first thing I did was to gather a group of the most creative people at school to help me.*

*I held a meeting where the group and I came up with every idea we could think of to advertise the concert and get people talking about it. Some of the ideas seemed kind of crazy at first, but when we discussed them we saw ways we could make them work.*

*One unique thing we did was to come up with a slogan and a logo for the concert. We also used bright orange on all our flyers and posters to make the concert stick in people's minds. We even made orange T-shirts, buttons, and stickers with the logo and slogan that we sold before the show to raise additional money.*

*To get people from outside the school to buy tickets and come to the concert, we dressed all in orange and passed out flyers at malls and movie theaters. (We made sure we asked permission from the mall and theater management before we did this.) I even painted my face orange. We got so much attention that we made it on to the local evening news!*

*We ended up selling out the concert and raising a lot of money for the hurricane victims. We also showed the adults that we could do anything we set our minds to.*

# Build Your Skills

**T**hinking creatively is a skill you can develop over time. Be on the lookout for opportunities in your education and activities that will encourage you to think in new ways.

## Education

- Start a brand new club at school. Think of something that interests you that's never been tried. Think of creative activities for the club to pursue.

- Ask your teachers to suggest fiction books that imagine entirely different realities, such as science fiction or fantasy books.

- Study art as a way to express your creativity. Take a class in painting or sculpture and use color and shapes to explore an idea. Every piece of art is original because it comes from a unique individual, and coming up with original things requires creative thinking.

## Activities

- Learn how to make something, such as woodworking or pottery. When you are learning something new, you haven't yet learned all the old ways of doing things, so your mind is freer to think up new approaches.

- When you have a problem to solve, put aside all your preconceptions and start from scratch. Don't think about why you can't try a certain approach, think what would happen if you did.

- Explore different ways of thinking about things by browsing the Internet. Join discussion groups and ask others how they would approach a problem. Note how many different answers you get. People can be very creative!

## Try It Yourself

You have a summer job working at a doughnut cart at the local farmers' market every Saturday morning. Your boss tells you that sales have fallen off from last year, and asks you to think of ways to get sales up again.

Follow these steps to put your creative thinking skills to work:

1. Think up new flavors of doughnuts that might attract people. Ask customers what they'd like to try, check out other doughnut flavors at local bakeries, and then come up with a new flavor. Don't be timid: how about pineapple walnut, pumpkin chocolate, or Parmesan and bacon doughnuts?

2. Come up with a promotional idea. Try a doughnut-flavor-of-the-week promotion or provide kids with food coloring to paint their own faces on donuts.

3. Create a way to partner with another food vendor. Could the coffee cart and the doughnut cart give discounts to people who buy both coffee and a doughnut, for example?

4. Think of a creative pricing scheme. Bakeries typically give discounts for a dozen doughnuts, but how about giving a discount for half a dozen, or even three?

Creative thinking means being willing to try new things. It means coming up with new combinations and daring options. Try using brainstorming to get creative; get together with other people and have everybody throw out ideas, no matter how crazy. You'll be surprised at what you come up with.

# Performance Review

**W**hat rating would an employer give you on your creative thinking skills?

- Needs Improvement
- Average

- Above Average
- Outstanding

Take action to improve your ability to think creatively by using the methods in the following checklist.

---

## THINKING CREATIVELY CHECKLIST

○ Focus on putting aside preexisting ideas and keeping your mind open.

○ Try different combinations of ideas. Can you find connections between things that other people don't?

○ Look for new solutions to existing problems.

○ Express your ideas in creative ways, such as a story, a 3-D model, or a multimedia presentation.

---

# Words at Work

**T**hese words relate to thinking creatively. How many can you define?

- Visualize
- Imagine
- Preconceived
- Possibilities

- Fantasize
- Out-of-the-box
- Unique
- Brainstorming

# MAKING DECISIONS

The ability to make decisions is an important skill. But how do you make the right decision? Though you will sometimes make the wrong choice, if you can identify your goal, and then examine all the options and weigh the risks of each, you have a better chance of making more good decisions than bad. To be an effective decision maker, you also have to be willing to commit to the decisions you make.

The skill of making decisions includes the ability to

- Identify a goal and its constraints
- Determine what options are available
- Consider risks
- Evaluate and choose the best option

## Careers That Use This Skill

Any worker will do better by having this skill, but these careers are strongly focused on making decisions:

- Judges
- Military leaders
- Purchasing agents
  - Financial managers
  - Coaches
- Nurses
- Education administrators
- Interior designers
- Childcare workers
- Construction managers

# Why Employers Want This Skill

**P**eople in the workplace are called on to make dozens of decisions every day. You may have to make decisions about important business strategies. Perhaps you are the one to choose the brand of computer to buy for the office. Maybe you decide how much to spend on advertising your auto repair shop in the local paper.

Whatever the nature of the decision, being able to make it without delay is important. Some people hesitate about committing to one choice or another. They can't weigh the pros and cons of the available options easily. In the workplace, an employee's inability to make decisions can cost a company in terms of missed opportunities or wrong choices.

People who can make decisions quickly and with conviction (a strong belief in their choice) often move ahead in their careers. They are given more responsibility and opportunity. Most managers and leaders in business are good decision makers.

Making decisions means being willing to take some risks, but they should be informed risks. That means you should gather all available information and options and then do the best you can. You have the opportunity of making decisions about your life every day, so practice good decision-making skills now. That way you'll make a solid investment in your future career success.

> **❝**If I had to sum up in one word what makes a good manager, I'd say decisiveness.**❞**
> —Lee Iacocca, business executive

# Making Decisions on the Job

Name: Lisa Newborn

Job: Manager of a small craft business

*I run a small Internet business selling crafts my friends and I make in our crafts club. We donate the money we earn to the local animal shelter. Last summer, we started talking about creating some holiday-themed crafts and selling them through a larger online business. We thought we might use the extra money to make a big donation to the new animal shelter building drive.*

*Before making any decisions about the holiday crafts, I met with the rest of the club to talk about our goals. We set a goal for how much we wanted to make from the holiday crafts and talked about how we wanted to spend the extra money. Instead of giving all the profit to the shelter, some of my friends suggested using the additional money to travel to a nearby crafts show or donating it to another charity.*

*We also had to consider the risks involved with expanding the business and getting involved with another online company. What if the company we dealt with wasn't honest? What if we couldn't produce enough products to fill the orders? I also had to evaluate the amount of time I'd need to spend to keep the Web site going and process orders.*

*In the end, we decided to go for it. My friend Cherie did some research and found a reliable online store that we partnered with to sell our crafts. To help us meet the demand for the holiday crafts, we recruited more members. We decided against traveling to the craft show. Instead, we decided to give some of our profits to national animal charities as well as the local shelter.*

# Build Your Skills

**Y**ou can develop your ability to make decisions by taking advantage of educational and extracurricular opportunities.

### Education

- Take courses in business and management to learn about methods businesspeople use to make decisions.

- Study history to see what important decisions worked out well and which ones failed. Try to understand why some decisions are better than others.

### Activities

- Take on a leadership position in a club or group that requires you to make some choices for the members, such as how to spend money or what activities to pursue.

- When you are faced with decisions, take the time to analyze the situation, weigh the risks, and evaluate any alternatives. If a decision doesn't work out, try to figure out how you might have made a better decision and use that knowledge to help you make a better choice next time.

> **❝** *Intuitive decision making and mastering this profession are one and the same.* **❞**
> —Van Riper, former president of Marine Corps University

# Try It Yourself

You run errands for a small bakery after work. One day the top baker, your boss, leaves early. You get a call from a customer who needs a rush order of three dozen cookies for the next morning at 10. Follow these steps to put your decision-making skills to work:

1. Identify the goal. You want to make the customer happy and get the money for the business, but you know that if the baker can't get the order done in time, the customer will be unhappy.

2. Come up with alternatives. You could commit to the order and leave the baker, who comes into work at four in the morning, a note. You could tell the customer you can't commit to the order because the baker has left. Or you could try calling the baker at home and get back to the customer.

3. Evaluate the risks and benefits of each alternative. If you just leave a note and the baker gets in and can't handle the order, the customer will be disappointed. If he can do the order, everybody will be happy. If you say no to the customer, that customer may not order from the bakery again. On the other hand, you don't risk disappointing the customer by failing to get the cookies done. If you call the baker at home, he might get angry with you for disturbing him, or he might be grateful you worked so hard to keep a customer happy. Use what you know about the baker to help you evaluate your options.

4. Make the decision! Delaying the customer by being indecisive will make the customer feel frustrated.

# Performance Review

**W**hat rating would an employer give you on your ability to make decisions?

- Needs Improvement
- Average
- Above Average
- Outstanding

To improve your rating, always follow the process outlined in the following checklist when you make important decisions.

## MAKING DECISIONS CHECKLIST

- ◯ Identify the goal you are trying to reach.
- ◯ Create a few possible alternatives that would help you reach that goal.
- ◯ Consider the risks and possible benefits of each alternative.
- ◯ Evaluate the alternatives and come to a decision.
- ◯ Stick to your decision and see it through.

# Words at Work

**T**hese words relate to making decisions. How many can you define?

- Alternatives
- Conviction
- Constraint
- Goals
- Risk
- Opportunity
- Evaluate
- Decisive

# SOLVING PROBLEMS

**P**roblems are a fact of life. They occur when things don't proceed the way you expected or wanted them to. The ability to solve problems and move forward is important in many jobs and in life.

The first step to solving any problem is to recognize that you have one. You have to see that there is a difference between what is happening and what should be happening. But you can't stop there! Solving problems also includes the ability to

- Identify possible reasons for the problem
- Think of a plan of action to solve the problem and carry it out
- Determine how the plan is working
- Change the plan as necessary to improve results

## Careers That Use This Skill

**A**ny worker will do better by having this skill, but these careers are strongly focused on solving problems on a regular basis:

- Lawyers
- Police
- Auto mechanics
- Computer support specialists
- Hotel managers
- Engineers
- Childcare workers
- Counselors
- Repairers
- Customer service representatives

# Why Employers Want This Skill

**I**n your work, you will have to depend on many things going right: people avoiding making mistakes, equipment functioning as it should, deliveries being made on time, and so on. But things don't always go right. Machinery breaks down, materials don't arrive on time, or the computer network crashes. When something doesn't go as you expected, you have a problem.

If you are good at identifying problems, figuring out their cause, and devising a plan of action to fix the problem, you will be able to complete your work successfully. If you aren't good at solving problems, they could stop you from completing your work or could cause you to do a poor job.

Not every change at work is a problem, however. Sometimes you need to adapt rather than solve something. But when something seems like a problem, research its cause, see whether you can make a change happen, and look for the best way to make that change. Employers look for employees who can solve problems on their own without constantly having to ask for help. Employers also tend to have a lot of confidence in these kinds of employees.

> **"**An undefined problem has an infinite number of solutions.**"**
> —Robert A. Humphrey

# Solving Problems on the Job

Name: Carrie Winters

Job: Paper carrier

*I have a newspaper route in my neighborhood. When I started the route, the papers were dropped off at my front curb around 4 p.m. every day, but after several months they started arriving at 5 p.m.*

*At first, I just adjusted my schedule to make my deliveries later. But then Mr. Obermeyer complained to me that his paper was coming late. Also, my stepmom thought it would be dangerous for me to ride my bike around the neighborhood that late when it got dark out earlier in winter. Delivering the papers later also meant that I missed eating dinner with my family.*

*I finally contacted the newspaper to find out the reason for the change. I asked whether it was temporary or permanent. My supervisor said the newspaper had to get rid of some of the delivery trucks to save money, so 5 p.m. would be the new schedule.*

*I thought about what I could do to solve the problems. I decided to change my delivery route so that Mr. Obermeyer would get his paper at the time he had been used to. I also bought a light for my bike and some reflective tape for my jacket so that I would be safer riding in the dark. It worked out okay for a while, but I started to miss the time I used to have in the evening at home. I called the paper back and arranged to have a shorter route. I don't make as much money, but the new route works out better for me.*

# Build Your Skills

**A**re you willing to tackle problems in your daily life or at school? Or do you tend to give up and leave the solution to somebody else? The more you tackle problems, the more practice you get in problem solving. There are many ways you can develop this important skill.

## Education

- Take math classes to learn how to approach problems with a certain logical method.
- Read about business management to learn successful approaches to solving problems.
- Look for examples of problem solving by your teachers and principal.

## Activities

- Think of a plan to correct a problem in your life right now. Put the plan into action and see whether it works. Change the plan if necessary.
- Identify a problem in the world today such as a war or a medical condition without a known cure. Research what people have done to try to solve this problem. What's worked? What hasn't?
- Suggest a problem scenario to several people and ask how they would solve it. You might be surprised how many different suggestions you get. Which is the best? Could two or more of the suggestions work, even thought they use a different approach?

## Try It Yourself

Your grandmother's shift at work has changed, and she's no longer available to drive you to your piano lessons on Thursday afternoons. Follow these steps to put your problem-solving skills to work:

1. Identify the problem. In this case, the problem is one of both transportation and timing.

2. Identify the possible reasons for the problem. You could look at the problem as being your grandmother's schedule, the timing of your lesson, or the challenge of transportation.

3. Consider all the possible solutions. Look at the three possible reasons listed in step 2. Each reason suggests a solution. First, your grandmother could change her schedule. Second, you could change the timing of your lesson to a day and time when she can drive you. Third, you could find another mode of transportation, such as a bus or having another relative drive you.

4. Pick the solution that seems most promising. If your grandmother can't change her schedule, you can rule out that solution. If there is no other transportation, your only option is to reschedule the lesson.

5. Implement and monitor the solution. Talk to your piano teacher and find a new time for your lesson. Make sure that time works for your grandmother, too. If it ends up being inconvenient, you may have to go back and figure out another solution.

# Performance Review

**W**hat rating would an employer give you on solving problems?

- Needs Improvement
- Average
- Above Average
- Outstanding

To become an outstanding problem solver, keep the items on the following checklist in mind when you're faced with a problem.

---

## SOLVING PROBLEMS CHECKLIST

- ⭘ Determine whether there is a problem and what the reasons for that problem are.

- ⭘ Come up with a good plan to solve the problem.

- ⭘ Evaluate whether the plan is working and be willing to try a different one if it isn't.

---

# Words at Work

**T**hese words relate to problem solving. How many can you define?

- Discrepancy
- Solution
- Resolve
- Evaluate
- Strategy
- Monitor
- Modify
- Implement
- Approach

# VISUALIZING

**B**eing able to visualize means that you can see things in your mind's eye that may not exist yet. For example, you may be able to look at a design for a house and visualize what the rooms will look like inside when it's built. The ability to visualize is something like having a good imagination.

Visualizing includes the ability to

- Organize and process symbols, graphs, pictures, and objects
- Understand the flow of work from a description
- Imagine the results of building something by studying a blueprint, diagram, or other document
- Anticipate the effect of an action before you take it

## Careers That Use This Skill

**A**ny worker will do better by having this skill, but these careers are strongly focused on being able to visualize or imagine a finished product:

- Engineers
- Architects
- Fashion designers
- Musicians
- Artists
- Writers
- CADD operators
- Historians
- Appliance repair people
- Urban planners
- Hairstylists

# Why Employers Want This Skill

Employers use the skill of visualizing in a couple of ways. First, some specific job-related tasks require visualization. For example, a project manager may look at a diagram that shows the flow of work in a project and be able to imagine how the tasks of the project will occur. Or an accountant might read a graph and be able to see a financial trend. All kinds of jobs use this skill, from a chef who can imagine what a recipe will taste like before making it to an engineer who can read a schematic for a robot and tell you what that robot can do. Second, being able to visualize helps any worker to come up with possible solutions to all kinds of problems and to come up with new and better ways of getting things done. Visualizing helps you examine solutions to problems before you put them in place so you can choose the right course of action before you spend too much time and money.

Employers hiring for a job that requires visualization may test that ability by asking a person to read a diagram or graph or to show a degree or certification in a field such as architecture or engineering. Some job interviewers will ask questions that challenge you to solve a proposed problem. Your answers to these questions can indicate how well you can visualize. Whether or not the career you want to explore requires job-related visualization tasks, being able to imagine possible outcomes will improve your performance on almost any job.

> **"** I visualize things in my mind before I have to do them. It is like having a mental workshop. **"**
> —Jack Youngblood, athlete

# Visualizing on the Job

Name: Stacy Newman

Job: Delivery person

*I help my sister with her business by delivering cosmetics to people in the neighborhood on my bike. I sometimes have to ride several miles to make the deliveries. I use a map to figure out the most efficient route to all the houses. I have to visualize not only the route but also the terrain (terrain means the shape of the land—some spots have lots of hills to ride up, for example) from my memory. I must imagine how long it will take to ride to each house and make each delivery to plan a schedule for the day that gets me home before dark. I also have to figure out how many packages I can fit in my basket and the best way to arrange the packages.*

*Every year just before Christmas there is always one long day of delivering to all the regular customers. I like helping on this day, because the customers often give me little Christmas gifts. Of course I then have to visualize how I will solve the problem of transporting the gifts I get along the way if my basket is still very full.*

> **"** The entrepreneur is essentially a visualizer and an actualizer. **"**
> —Robert L. Schwartz, law professor

# Build Your Skills

**V**isualizing is a skill you can develop over time through your education and activities.

## Education

- Take courses in art to help you understand things in a visual way. Courses in music also help you to imagine music from reading note symbols.

- Classes in shop and science often require you to study a concept or process and visualize its outcome.

- When you read books in English classes, use the descriptions to help you visualize the settings and characters.

## Activities

- Join a club that builds things from drawings or diagrams, such as electronics or woodworking.

- Practice describing or writing about your own experiences. Part of visualizing is being able to explain what you see in your mind's eye to others, so work on developing a good, descriptive vocabulary.

- Study paintings and other types of fine art to see how artists have visualized certain ideas.

- If you have a career interest such as architecture or mathematics, study the symbols used to represent various items in those career fields.

- Use software to create visual representations of objects. For example, practice creating charts in spreadsheet software to represent sets of numbers, or learn to draw blueprints of rooms in your house in a drawing program.

# Try It Yourself

**Y**ou've volunteered to coordinate the sewing of costumes for the annual school play. This year the play takes place in Victorian England. Follow these steps to put your visualizing skills to work:

1. Find examples of Victorian costumes. Search on the Internet, or look in your local library for books on costumes.

2. Consider how the colors you use in the costumes will look onstage. Meet with the set designer to see drawings of the set and consider which characters will be onstage together; you don't want their costumes to clash! For practice, look up sets online for plays set in Victorian England.

3. Begin to imagine how each costume will look. Draw sketches and attach fabric swatches to them. This combination will help you imagine how each costume will look when it is created with that fabric.

4. Create a timetable for construction of costumes. Picture the details of each costume. Visualize in your mind's eye how long it will take to make each costume. Then consider how much time you and helpers have every day to work on them. Finally, write down a work diagram that lists each task to be done and determine how much overall time will be needed to complete the costumes.

Visualizing involves thinking things through, not just getting an instant image of something in your mind. To visualize an outcome, you have to organize the details in your mind. You can use tools such as diagrams, sketches, calendars, and maps to turn your ideas into concrete plans.

# Performance Review

**W**hat rating would an employer give you on visualizing?

- Needs Improvement
- Average
- Above Average
- Outstanding

Take action to earn an Outstanding rating by working on the tasks in the following checklist.

---

## VISUALIZING CHECKLIST

○ Organize information in your mind.

○ Read a graph, chart, picture, or set of symbols and understand the overall meaning being conveyed.

○ Think of possible solutions and imagine possible outcomes without trying out each solution first.

○ Imagine sounds, smells, and tastes just from a verbal description of them.

---

# Words at Work

**T**hese words relate to visualizing. How many can you define?

- Vision
- Imagine
- Mind's eye
- Envisage
- Envision
- Concept
- Schematic
- Description

# KNOWING HOW TO LEARN

Everybody has the capacity to learn, but some people know learning techniques that help them learn more quickly or thoroughly. Some learning skills come naturally to people. For example, a visual learner will pick up new information easily if he or she is shown the information in pictures or diagrams. Understanding what kind of learner you are can help you learn new things throughout your life. Try to figure out your learning style. Knowing how to learn includes the ability to

- Recognize and use learning techniques
- Apply and adapt new knowledge in familiar and changing situations
- Use knowledge of learning styles and strategies

## Careers That Use This Skill

Any worker will do better by having this skill, but some careers are strongly focused on being able to learn new information regularly:

- Tax attorneys
- Computer software developers
  - Teachers
  - Musicians
- Technical writers
- Real estate agents
- Construction managers
- Doctors
- Police
- Actors and actresses

# Why Employers Want This Skill

**E**mployees in just about any career have to learn new things all the time. They have to learn company procedures and systems, which change on a regular basis. They also have to learn new information about their jobs. For example, an auto mechanic has to learn how to work on new car models, a doctor has to keep up with advances in medicine, and an administrative assistant has to learn new software programs.

Employers spend a lot of money on training people in these areas. People who learn things quickly take less time to train, meaning that the company's training costs are lower and these people can get to work with their new skills more quickly.

In addition, if you develop good learning skills, you can adapt things you learned before to new situations. In effect, you teach yourself without anybody having to train you.

> **"**Only the curious will learn and only the resolute overcome the obstacles to learning. The quest quotient has always excited me more than the intelligence quotient. **"**
> —Eugene S. Wilson, Dean of Admissions for Amherst College

# Knowing How to Learn on the Job

Name: Hannah Goldberg

Job: Food server

*I started a part-time job as a waitress in a local restaurant a couple months ago. I was a little bit nervous because I'd never been a waitress before and there was a lot to learn.*

*I learn best through pictures, so I asked the hostess to give me a copy of the diagram of the dining room that she uses when she's seating people. Studying that diagram helped me to remember the table locations and their numbers.*

*My manager told me to follow Nadine around on my first day so that she could show me the ropes. (She has worked at the restaurant for three years.) I kept a small notebook and pen to write down the important things she told me so that I wouldn't forget them.*

*It took me about a week to learn all the menu items. I started by learning the side items because that's what the customers seemed to have the most questions about. Clustering the like items together helped me learn the menu faster.*

*When I first started waiting tables, it helped me to think of the times when I helped my mother serve a big holiday dinner. I had to do the same sorts of things. I had to fill all the drinks and get any extras people needed from the kitchen. I also tried to anticipate what people would need so I didn't make so many trips. For example, if a customer ordered barbecued ribs, he would also need extra napkins. (I remember my little brother always needed extra napkins no matter what he was eating.) I also made sure that I always was polite.*

# Build Your Skills

**K**nowing how to learn new things is a skill you can develop over time through your education and activities.

## Education

- Take courses in education in college to discover different learning techniques.

- Pay attention to how you learn in different classes and with different teachers. What works? What doesn't?

- Take courses that require you to learn not just facts, but procedures. For example, take an auto repair course or a cooking class.

## Activities

- Join a club such as Future Teachers of America that involves people interested in teaching and approaches to learning.

- Enter a mentoring relationship. For example, volunteer with a literacy group to help somebody learn to read. When you teach, you discover a lot about how people learn.

- Learn something completely new such as how to read music or speak a foreign language. Notice which learning techniques work for you and which don't.

- Read a book about learning styles and techniques. Can you identify which of your friends learn in which style?

> **"**Learning is not attained by chance. It must be sought for with ardor and attended to with diligence.**"**
> —Abigail Adams, a First Lady of the United States

# Try It Yourself

Your cat has had kittens that were born prematurely. Your foster mother has asked you to take care of them, but you don't know how. She helps you with some advice, but you decide to learn more about what you should do. Follow these steps to put your learning skills to work:

1. Search the Internet for information about newborn kittens and their needs. Note that some search engines let you look for images instead of print articles. If you're a visual learner, try the visual images!

2. Ask for a demonstration. If your foster mother has experience with newborn kittens, ask her to show you once or twice how to take care of them. Once you get the hang of it, you can take over!

3. Consider skills you already have that you can adapt to this situation. Did you help to take care of a younger brother or sister or baby-sit a younger child at some point? What did you learn then that you could use now?

4. Are there learning tools such as video programs or online animated demonstrations available? Be open to using the latest technologies in your learning. Many tools provide useful learning techniques.

When you learn new things, you should use any and all resources at hand. You may find that you can memorize a list of information by putting it to music or rhyming it. Do whatever works for you to learn, and enjoy this remarkable experience!

# Performance Review

**W**hat rating would an employer give you on knowing how to learn?

- Needs Improvement
- Average
- Above Average
- Outstanding

Use the methods in the following checklist to become an outstanding learner.

## KNOWING HOW TO LEARN CHECKLIST

- ◯ Apply and adapt new information to changing situations.
- ◯ Use learning tools and strategies to learn more effectively.
- ◯ Be aware of what kind of learner you are.
- ◯ Group information in clusters to help you remember it.

# Words at Work

**T**hese words relate to knowing how to learn. How many can you define?

- Recognize
- Learning styles
- Clustering
- Assumptions
- Conclusions
- Awareness
- Adapt
- Strategy

# REASONING

Some people define reason as the ability to think. When you try to figure out a problem, you use your reasoning skills. Reasoning involves the use of logic. Logic is applying rules and tests to ideas and facts to draw conclusions that make sense.

Believe or not, you can learn how to think. You can learn methods of applying your thinking skills to problems or situations that will help you come to the most logical conclusion possible.

Reasoning skills include the ability to

- Discover a rule or principle underlying the relationship between two or more objects
- Apply rules to solve a problem
- Form conclusions from available information by using logic
- Determine which conclusions are correct given a set of facts and conclusions

## Careers That Use This Skill

Any worker will do better by having this skill, but these careers are strongly focused on using reasoning skills on a regular basis:

- Scientists
- Engineers
- Financial analysts
- Economists
- Judges
- Detectives
- Psychologists
- Reporters
- Archaeologists
- Repairers

# Why Employers Want This Skill

**S**olving problems and drawing conclusions to act on is part of every job. Everybody is presented with facts daily and must find relationships among them that suggest a course of action. Accountants conclude that a certain tax law would make sense in their client's situation. Salespeople consider a customer's needs and budget and the products they have to offer, and they come up with a logical fit.

People who aren't very good at applying reason to a situation aren't necessarily unintelligent. They may just lack experience or tools for making decisions and coming to conclusions in a logical way. Employers value those who can reason well because they are good at making decisions, solving problems, and getting things done based on logical thinking.

> **"**The grand aim of all science is to cover the greatest number of empirical facts by logical deduction from the smallest number of hypotheses. **"**
> —Eugene S. Wilson, Dean of Admissions for Amherst College

# Reasoning on the Job

Name: Evan Bronkhurst

Job: Skateboard factory worker

*During my summer break from engineering school, I have been working in a small factory that makes skateboards. One day I was on a lunch break in the picnic area behind the factory, and Mr. Vasquez, my supervisor, came out of the building. He looked worried and told me that in the last week they had a lot of problems with the skateboards being wobbly.*

*After lunch, Mr. Vasquez pulled me and a couple of other guys from the production line to help him figure out what the problem was. First we made a list of all the possible causes; we even included some that weren't that likely. We made sure to include any changes that happened to the parts or procedures around the time the problem started.*

*Then we narrowed down the list to the most probable causes and tested those options. We used the data from the tests to draw the most logical conclusion about the cause. When something we tried didn't turn out to be the cause, we went back to the list and tried the next group of options. We tried to keep an open mind so that we didn't rule out a possible cause too quickly.*

*The cause behind the wobbly skateboards turned out to be a combination of things. We found out that the wheels in the last shipment that the factory received from the wheel supplier were defective. Also, the employees who installed the wheels weren't taking the time to check the wheels before installation because they were trying to make as many skateboards as they could to meet the monthly goal.*

# Build Your Skills

**R**easoning is a skill you can develop over time through your educational experiences and other activities.

### Education

- Take courses in science and mathematics. These subjects will help you learn how to apply reasoning methods to draw conclusions about various kinds of known information.

- Study management techniques to learn how managers make decisions and draw conclusions.

### Activities

- Read a book about a scientist who made a major discovery and note how this person worked through various options and came to a conclusion.

- Next time you have a problem, sit down and make a list of possible options and methodically think about them until you can choose the best one.

- Study historical conclusions that were faulty. How did people come to that conclusion? For example, at one time people thought that the world was flat. Why? What changed their minds?

> **❝**Chance favors the prepared mind.**❞**
> —Louis Pasteur, scientist

# Try It Yourself

**Y**our computer keeps crashing while you're trying to do your homework. How can you use reasoning to figure out the problem? Follow these steps to put your reasoning skills to work:

1. Try to determine whether anybody has made a change to the computer that could have caused the problem. Has anybody installed new software or downloaded a large file? Windows-based computers enable you to do a system restore that takes you back to the settings you had before you started having the problem.

2. Look at what you are trying to use the computer for tonight. Are you doing something different than you've done before that's causing the problem? If your homework tonight involves working with large graphics files, for example, there may be an issue with your graphics driver, or your computer might not have enough memory to handle the files.

3. Restart the computer and see whether this action solves the problem. Sometimes stopping and then restarting machines that power up causes them to reset themselves, which solves the problem.

4. Gather any information you can that might help you. Check the system information, look at how much memory is being used, and use the help system.

Reasoning is simply applying some order to the way you think about things. You consider all possibilities, then focus on the likeliest, and then work your way through the facts to come to a conclusion. You can apply reasoning to any situation.

# Performance Review

**W**hat rating would an employer give you on your reasoning skills?

- Needs Improvement
- Average
- Above Average
- Outstanding

To earn an Outstanding rating, do the tasks in the following checklist when you are faced with a problem.

---

## REASONING CHECKLIST

○ Apply the rules and principles you already know to the situation.

○ Use logic to draw conclusions from known facts.

○ Determine which conclusions are correct based on the facts you are given.

---

# Words at Work

**T**hese words relate to reasoning. How many can you define?

- Assumptions
- Conclusions
- Awareness
- Principle
- Logic
- Facts
- Discover
- Methodology

# BEING RESPONSIBLE

Being responsible means that you answer for your actions. If you say you will do something, you do it. If you make a mistake, you admit it and face the consequences.

As you grow up, you will have more freedom to do what you choose to do. No teacher or parent will be around to make you be responsible. You have to learn to take responsibility for your own life.

Being responsible includes the ability to

- Work hard to reach a goal
- Set high standards in order to achieve excellence
- Pay attention to details and concentrate on a task
- Show up on time
- Be enthusiastic and optimistic while working on tasks

## Careers That Use This Skill

Any worker will do better by having this skill, but these careers are strongly focused on being responsible:

- Doctors
- Astronauts
- Air traffic controllers
- Police
- Pilots
- Truck drivers
- Paramedics
- Dentists
- Social workers
- Inspectors
- Childcare workers
- Animal care workers
- Aircraft technicians

# Why Employers Want This Skill

All employers expect a basic level of responsibility from their employees. For example, employers expect their employees to show up when they are scheduled to work. People who are not responsible may show up late or not show up at all. This lack of responsibility is a major reason people are fired from jobs.

Employers also expect employees to do the job they are assigned. Responsible people don't just do the minimum; they take pride in doing a job well. They have high standards for their work and do what it takes to complete a job. Responsible people also show enthusiasm for their work, and employers appreciate this positive attitude. For these reasons, people with a strong sense of responsibility are more likely to succeed at work.

Being responsible also rewards the responsible person. That person can feel pride and a sense of accomplishment when a job is done well. Irresponsible people don't enjoy the same sense of pride in their work.

> **❝** The key to accepting responsibility for your life is to accept the fact that your choices, every one of them, are leading you inexorably to either success or failure. **❞**
>
> —Neal Boortz, radio talk show host

# Being Responsible on the Job

Name: Seth Thompson

Job: Part-time bookstore clerk

*I help out my mom on the weekends at her small bookstore downtown. I shelve the new books and take in books that people trade in for the used book section. Last Saturday around lunchtime, my mom had to leave suddenly because my grandmother fell. The fall wasn't serious, but Mom had to pick Grandma up from the doctor's office. That left just Charles, who works at the store full time, and me working in the store.*

*There weren't any customers in the store when Mom left, and it was almost time for Charles to take his lunch break. He needed to go out and get something to eat because he hadn't brought any lunch with him, but he promised to be gone only for half an hour. I was left in charge of the store.*

*I was hungry, too, but I knew I had to stay in the store no matter what. I couldn't leave until Charles or my mom came back. Customers started to come in then, and I worked hard to provide good service to everybody. Providing poor service to customers could cause them to stop coming to the store.*

*Being responsible can be hard. You have to set high standards for yourself, work hard, and not walk out on your work even if you are hungry or tired. The store was so busy that I stayed until closing time. My mom told me she was glad that she could count on me to do what needed to be done.*

# Build Your Skills

**B**eing responsible is a skill you can develop over time. Look for opportunities in your education and activities to be more responsible.

### Education

- Punctuality is a great habit to have, so focus on being on time to all your classes. Set a goal of going an entire semester without being tardy.

- Complete all of your assignments by the due date. Double-check your work before you hand it in to make sure that it is complete and shows your best work. Try to exceed your teacher's expectations.

### Activities

- Take on more responsibility at home by taking care of a pet, for example, or babysitting for a younger sibling. Show your family that you are responsible by completing assigned chores willingly and without needing to be reminded.

- Run for a position in student government or volunteer to head a committee in a club or group that you belong to. Part of being a good leader is accepting responsibility for the group and project you are in charge of. When you take on a task, be sure that you can commit the time, energy, and enthusiasm required to get the job done.

- Set high goals for yourself in school and in your extracurricular activities. Whether you are at soccer practice or in a piano lesson, concentrate on doing your personal best.

## Try It Yourself

**Y**ou start a pet-sitting business in the neighborhood. You go to people's houses and feed and walk dogs and take care of cats when folks are out of town. You can show that you are responsible in the following ways:

1. Get a contact number for the people who are out of town and a phone number for their veterinarian. If there is an emergency, you have to know how to handle it and where to get help. Being responsible means that you are in charge no matter what happens.

2. Always show up for work and be on time. If you can't make it for some reason, you should arrange for somebody else to take care of the pets.

3. Set high standards for your work and meet or exceed them. You could take care of pets by just feeding and walking them, but pets left alone for hours on end need more than that. If you want to be seen as a good pet sitter, you should also clean up any messes the pets have made, give them some play time, and offer them affection.

When you are responsible, you know the importance of completing your work and doing a good job. You follow through to make sure things are done and done well because your work reflects on you.

> **"**You cannot escape the responsibility of tomorrow by evading it today.**"**
> —Abraham Lincoln, U.S. President

# Performance Review

**W**hat rating would an employer give you on being responsible?

- Needs Improvement
- Average
- Above Average
- Outstanding

Take action to earn an Outstanding rating by consistently doing the tasks in the following checklist.

## BEING RESPONSIBLE CHECKLIST

- ◯ Work hard to achieve your goals.
- ◯ Set high standards for yourself and meet them.
- ◯ Concentrate on getting the job done, even when the job is unpleasant.
- ◯ Do what you say you will do.
- ◯ Show excitement when you have to tackle and complete tasks.

# Words at Work

**T**hese words relate to responsibility. How many can you define?

- Persevere
- Standards
- Concentration
- Attendance
- Punctuality
- Enthusiasm
- Optimism
- Follow-through

# HAVING SELF-ESTEEM

Esteem means to have respect for or set a value on someone or something. Having self-esteem means that you have respect for yourself and understand your own value. Self-esteem doesn't mean that you think you are better than others. The trick to having self-esteem is to have a realistic view of your own abilities. People with strong self-esteem often have a positive view towards others as well because they are not threatened by the success of others.

The various aspects to having self-esteem include

- Maintaining a positive view of yourself
- Demonstrating knowledge of your skills and abilities
- Being aware of the impact you have on others
- Knowing how to deal with your emotions

## Careers That Use This Skill

Any worker will do better by having this skill, but people in these careers greatly benefit from having self-esteem:

- Athletes
- Air traffic controllers
- Firefighters
- Surgeons
- Pilots
- Lawyers
- Artists
- Actors and actresses
- Inventors

# Why Employers Want This Skill

**E**mployers appreciate employees with self-esteem because they have a realistic confidence in their abilities. They don't make claims to abilities they don't have. They are willing to try to learn new things because they believe in their own ability to do so.

People with self-esteem don't waste time worrying about what they can't do. Instead they forge ahead and take on challenges, knowing that if they don't have the skills to succeed, they can acquire them. People with self-esteem are able to ask for help when they need it. Because they are confident, they don't feel that needing help reduces them in others' eyes.

Employees with self-esteem seldom need employers to hold their hands. They are capable of working on their own without constant attention or praise from others. Finally, people with self-esteem are less likely to show disrespect for themselves by abusing drugs or alcohol, which can affect their work.

Having self-esteem tends to make you more successful no matter what career you choose. It will also help you advance in any profession.

> **❝** The feeling that 'I am enough' does not mean that I have nothing to learn, nothing further to achieve, and nowhere to grow to. It means I accept, value, and respect myself. **❞**
> —**Hasidic saying**

# Having Self-Esteem on the Job

Name: Marcia Vasquez

Job: School bake sale volunteer

*I often make cookies for the annual school bake sale. This year, the principal asked me to organize the sale. My teacher, Mrs. Hodiak, helped me, but I was in charge.*

*I had to rely on my self-confidence quite a bit to tackle this job. I had experience in baking for the sale and had attended the sale for the last few years. I used the experience I already had with the sale to help me organize it. However, there were some parts of the sale that I didn't know that much about, so I asked Mrs. Hodiak and other volunteers for help with those areas. I listened to all their advice and information and used it to make decisions that I could feel good about.*

*Even when there were problems, I tried to stay positive and not stress out too much. I think my positive attitude helped the other volunteers relax and have fun while they worked at the sale. Even though I had never been in charge of a bake sale before, I knew I could make it a success. I think one of the reasons the principal asked me to organize the sale was that he knows that I'm not afraid to take on new challenges or learn new things.*

> **"**The man who has confidence in himself gains the confidence of others. **"**
> —Nathaniel Brandon, psychotherapist

# Build Your Skills

$S$elf-esteem is something you can develop over time through your education and other activities.

### Education

- Take classes in your area of interest so that you can have confidence in your abilities when you enter the job market.

- Approach challenging assignments with confidence. Usually the worst thing that can happen if you fail isn't all that bad, so don't dwell on the negative, but on the opportunity for success and growth.

### Activities

- Test your skills in a competition. Practicing for and participating in a competition is a good way to get a clear view of what your strengths are.

- Volunteer your skills. Are you good in math? Offer to tutor younger kids who are struggling with that subject. Do you like to build things? Sign up to help with a local Habitat for Humanity project. Using your skills to help someone else will help you to feel good about yourself.

- Spend time with your friends. Good friends like you for who you are, and they are happy for you when you do well. They know just what to say when you are feeling bad about yourself, and they can put you in your place if you start thinking too much of yourself. Remember that people who make you participate in self-destructive behavior or feel bad about yourself are not your friends.

# Try It Yourself

You get the leading role in the community theater musical. The role requires you to do some dancing. Though you know you have a good singing voice, you have never tried to dance. Here's how you can approach this challenge with self-esteem:

1. Feel confident in your acting and singing ability. These abilities will help you deliver a strong performance. Focusing on what you are good at can often provide the confidence to tackle areas where you have less skill.

2. Think about similar skills you may have that you can apply to learning to dance. Do you play tennis or swim? These and other sports require grace and balance. Build on what you already know and apply those abilities to new challenges.

3. Work hard to learn the new skill, feeling confident in your ability to take on new challenges. Most people can learn just about anything if they apply themselves. Some people have to work harder than others, but if they persevere and have confidence, they are likely to eventually succeed.

Having self-esteem gives you a very important tool to use in taking on new challenges and learning new skills. Those who have no self-esteem often give up without trying. One thing is sure: If you don't try, you will never succeed.

# Performance Review

What rating would an employer give you on having self-esteem?

- Needs Improvement
- Average
- Above Average
- Outstanding

Take action to earn an Outstanding rating by consistently doing the tasks in the following checklist.

---

## SELF-ESTEEM CHECKLIST

- ◯ Believe in yourself and your abilities.
- ◯ Keep a positive view about life and your ability to meet its challenges.
- ◯ Maintain a realistic awareness of your skills.
- ◯ Understand how you handle emotions.
- ◯ Have confidence in your ability to learn and grow.

---

# Words at Work

These words relate to self-esteem. How many can you define?

- Assurance
- Confidence
- Certainty
- Self-respect
- Self-worth
- Undaunted
- Poise
- Positive

# BEING SOCIABLE

**P**eople are social creatures. That means that they tend to come together in groups and seek out each other's company. Sociable people connect with other people and relate well to them. They try to understand what other people are feeling.

When you are sociable, you are comfortable interacting with other people. You make people feel that you like them and are interested in them. In turn, that makes people tend to like you.

Being sociable includes the ability to

- Show friendliness and politeness in a group
- Adapt to a variety of social settings
- Respond appropriately to social situations

## Careers That Use This Skill

**A**ny worker will do better by having this skill, but people in these careers greatly benefit from being sociable:

- Flight attendants
- Tour guides
- Real estate agents
- Waiters and waitresses
- Human resources specialists
- Receptionists
- Hotel clerks
- Veterinarians
- Public relations specialists
- Salespeople
- Insurance agents

# Why Employers Want This Skill

In most jobs people have to interact with others, whether with their boss, their coworkers, or with customers. Employers appreciate sociable people because these people know how to get along with others. In some jobs, such as sales or customer support, being able to connect with other people is part of the job description. In other jobs, sociability just helps them get along with the people they deal with on a daily basis.

People who aren't sociable may do fine in jobs where they work on their own most of the time. Still, some degree of sociability helps any employee to make and maintain healthy relationships with others. Sociable people typically are well-liked and don't get into fights with coworkers. They tend to be good communicators because they aren't nervous about speaking with others.

Sociable employees need to be careful not to take up too much of their work time socializing. After all, they must be able to complete their work. But when the situation is appropriate to socializing, the ability to do so can make a sale, earn a customer, or keep the morale of the office high.

> **"**Interdependence is and ought to be as much the ideal of man as self-sufficiency. Man is a social being.**"**
> —Mohandas Gandhi, political and spiritual leader

# Being Sociable on the Job

Name: Tyrese Collins

Job: School fund-raiser

*My school chorus made a CD of holiday songs to sell as a fund-raiser for a kid at school who is very sick. I'm pretty good with people, so I volunteered to go to a local business club meeting to talk about the CD and ask people to buy copies.*

*I spent time before the meeting talking to members and asking about their interests and the club's activities. I was friendly and polite. I introduced myself to people, shook their hands, and looked them in the eye when I spoke.*

*During my talk, I showed my interest in the club by commenting about some of its activities. After my talk, I took lots of orders for the CD, and some of the businesspeople gave me ideas for other groups I could contact. One woman even offered to sell the CD in her gift shop!*

*I know a lot of my friends would have a hard time talking to a bunch of adults like I did. It's true that the people in the group have more experience and money than I do. But they're people just like me, and I knew they would want to help. Once I showed an interest in who they were and what they were about, it was easy to get comfortable talking with them.*

# Build Your Skills

Being sociable is a skill you can develop over time through your education and activities.

## Education

- Take classes where you work closely with others. Performing arts classes such as band, choir, or acting provide the opportunity to work with larger groups. In science classes, you can work on experiments with a lab partner.

- To be able to connect with people, you have to be able to look at things from their point of view. While studying history, think about historical events from different points of view. Reading literature can also help you understand the feelings of others.

## Activities

- Join a club or participate in a team sport to learn how to function in groups.

- Make an effort to meet new people. Take the time to talk to them and learn about their interests and their backgrounds.

- Host a party. A party is a fun way to practice your manners and interact with your favorite people. Remember that the best hosts are good at making all the party guests feel comfortable.

- Networking is making connections with people in order to accomplish a goal, such as getting a job. Find out more about networking through the Internet or your local library. Can you use networking to help you reach your goals?

# Try It Yourself

**T**hough you are a bit shy, you are interested in working in politics and are running for the student council. You have to speak to different clubs and classes throughout your campaign. Here are a few tips for being sociable during your campaign:

1. Take the time to show an interest in others. Many people forget to ask others about themselves and really listen when they speak. You would be surprised how flattered people feel when you take the time to listen to them.

2. Show people that you understand their concerns. After you listen to people's ideas and problems, paraphrase (restate in your own words) what you've heard to show them you were listening. Find ways to show them that you understand their situation.

3. Be polite and friendly to everybody. To be politely sociable in a setting like a political campaign, you can't be nice to some people and not nice to others. Learn to look for things to appreciate in everyone you meet.

Being sociable doesn't mean that you are phony. You simply try to get to know and appreciate other people. You won't like everybody in the same way, but when you are in a social setting, try being friendly and at ease.

> **"**We take our bearings, daily, from others. To be sane is, to a great extent, to be sociable.**"**
> —**John Updike, writer**

## Performance Review

What rating would an employer give you on being sociable?

- Needs Improvement
- Average
- Above Average
- Outstanding

Take action to earn an Outstanding rating by doing the tasks in the following checklist.

---

### SOCIABILITY CHECKLIST

○ Be friendly and polite to people.

○ Show understanding to others and listen to what they say.

○ Assert yourself confidently in unfamiliar social settings.

○ Show an interest in other people.

○ Adapt to the expectations of others in a social group.

---

## Words at Work

These words relate to sociability. How many can you define?

- Etiquette
- Affable
- Empathetic
- Adaptable
- Compassionate
- Responsive
- Outgoing
- Paraphrase

# MANAGING YOURSELF

In school you are told what to study, when to go to a certain class, and what assignments you must do. As you get older and move into the working world, however, you will be more in control of your own time and actions. You may be given a set of responsibilities for the workday and told to deal with them the best you can. You will decide how much time to spend on each task, when to tackle each task, and how to complete each task.

Managing yourself includes the ability to

- Know what skills you have
- Set specific goals and track your progress
- Motivate yourself
- Respond to feedback without getting angry or upset

## Careers That Use This Skill

Any worker will do better by having this skill, but people in these careers need strong self-management skills:

- Painters
- Writers
- Managers
- Directors
- Truck drivers
- Plumbers
- Emergency medical technicians
- Electricians
- Maintenance workers

# Why Employers Want This Skill

**S**ome jobs are very structured, such as an assembly line worker who inserts one part into a machine all day long. Other jobs have general responsibilities, such as keeping the computer network running. These jobs have lots of duties and variety. For the most part, people in these jobs decide which tasks to perform and in what order to perform them.

When employers hire people for jobs with more responsibility, they look for people who are self-starters and who can figure out their own short- and long-term goals and plan how to achieve them. Self-managing people have a strong sense of responsibility and monitor their own progress. These types of employees usually meet their goals. This quality means that others in the company don't have to spend time watching over them.

Employers can trust self-managing people to get the job done, whether on their own or by asking for help when they need it. Employees with good self-management skills have a strong sense of responsibility and an awareness of their own skills and knowledge.

> **"** Be miserable. Or motivate yourself. Whatever has to be done, it's always your choice. **"**
> —Wayne Dyer, radio commentator and author

# Managing Yourself on the Job

Name: Stephen Redding

Job: Part-time worker at a travel agency

*My mother asked me to organize her small travel agency's receipts for the year to help her prepare to do her taxes. She needed the receipts organized and entered into the computer in the next two weeks.*

*The first thing I did was to set a goal for when to complete the task and figure out a schedule to meet the deadline. In order to set the schedule, I had to figure out what was involved in getting the job done. I had to go through a few envelopes containing receipts, divide them into piles by category, enter the individual receipt information into the computer program, and then print a report for my mother.*

*Part way through the job, I checked my progress to make sure I was on schedule. It was taking longer than I thought, so I told my mother how much of the job I had completed and asked her if I could have more time to complete the task. I also asked her to check what I had done so far to make sure I was doing things the way she wanted them done. When you're working on your own, it's important to know when to ask questions to make sure the job is done right and when to handle things by yourself.*

> **"** Goals provide the energy source that powers our lives. **"**
> —Dennis Waitley, productivity consultant

# Build Your Skills

You can learn how to manage yourself better through your education and activities.

### Education

- The next time you have a large project in school, be responsible for setting your goals, organizing your own work, and sticking to a schedule.

- Take courses or read about time management to improve the way you schedule your work.

- In college, you can take distance learning courses over your computer. With online courses you are responsible for organizing your own time and learning experience.

### Activities

- Identify a project you can do at home. For example, you might want to redecorate your room. Look at the individual steps to your goal, such as choosing paint colors, buying the paint, priming the walls, painting, and cleanup. Give yourself a deadline and manage your work to get it done on time.

- Is there some work your parents or teachers constantly have to remind you to do, such as taking out the garbage or handing in assignments? Determine to change your behavior so that nobody else has to remind you to do the work.

# Try It Yourself

During the two weeks of the state fair, your job is to help prepare the fairgrounds to open at 10 A.M. every day. This preparation involves washing down the tents, picking up trash, and connecting power cords. Follow these steps to put your self-management skills to work:

1.  You start work at 7:30 A.M. With two and a half hours to finish everything, you have to set a schedule. If you haven't done this work before, ask others how much time you should allow for each task. Monitor yourself to make sure you're not running behind.

2.  Figure out a logical sequence of work to meet your goals. Some others doing work at the same time as you are will need power, so connect the power cords first. Then, to allow the tents time to dry before people arrive, you might wash them next. Use logic to figure out the best order to complete your tasks.

3.  Create systems to help you do things efficiently. When you pick up trash, is there a way to avoid having to constantly go back all the way across the fairgrounds to one trash station? Could you set up two or three trash stations to save you time?

4.  If a problem occurs, try to handle it yourself. But if you can't handle something, be aware of your own limitations and ask for help. Employers count on you to alert them if there is a problem you can't solve.

# Performance Review

**W**hat rating would an employer give you on managing yourself?

- Needs Improvement
- Average
- Above Average
- Outstanding

Take action to earn an Outstanding rating by doing the tasks in the following checklist.

---

### MANAGING YOURSELF CHECKLIST

- ◯ Set goals and achieve them.
- ◯ Monitor your own progress and make changes if you're off track.
- ◯ Understand your own abilities.
- ◯ Motivate yourself to get to work and stick with it.
- ◯ Accept feedback and learn from it without feeling defensive.

---

# Words at Work

**T**hese words relate to managing yourself. How many can you define?

- Independent
- Critique
- Monitor
- Self-control
- Defensive
- Self-starter
- Restraint
- Assess

# BEING HONEST

Society views honesty as an important value. Honesty involves telling the truth as well as not performing dishonest acts such as stealing from others. Honesty and integrity often go hand in hand. Integrity means that you stick to a set of values. For example, if you believe that being late for work is wrong because you are cheating your employer, and so you are never late, you show integrity.

Being honest and having integrity include the ability to

- Recognize when a choice breaks with society's values
- Act in a way that matches your values
- Understand the impact of dishonest actions on yourself, others, and your organization
- Choose the ethical course of action

## Careers That Use This Skill

Any worker will do better by having this skill, but being honest is especially important in these careers:

- Police
- Bank tellers
- Security guards
- Stockbrokers
- Psychiatrists
- Accountants
- Cashiers
- Judges

# Why Employers Want This Skill

**E**mployers often state that honesty is the most important factor in hiring an employee. Employers have to trust employees to be honest with how they spend their time on the job, how they use the company equipment, and whether they take company supplies for their own use. Employees who are caught being dishonest are typically fired immediately.

Employers have to be able to trust their employees to handle information ethically and act in an honest way. For example, employees who take customer orders have access to credit card numbers and checking account numbers, and they are expected to keep that information safe and private. One dishonest employee could take that information and steal from a customer, which could leave the employer open to legal action.

You are expected to be honest in your work life in many large and small ways. Big acts of dishonesty, such as stealing from your employer, increase the employer's costs. But smaller acts of dishonesty affect employers as well. For example, if you call in sick when you are feeling well in order to get a day off, the rest of the employees end up having more work to do.

> **“**Underlying the whole scheme of civilization is the confidence men have in each other, confidence in their integrity, confidence in their honesty, confidence in their future. **”**
> —Bourke Cochran, Irish statesman

# Being Honest on the Job

Name: Sam Lee

Job: Box office worker

*I am in charge of the box office for the upcoming school play. The drama teacher, Mrs. Bray, gave me $50 to use to make change. I am also in charge of keeping track of the number of tickets sold. This accounting is the only way anyone knows how much money is collected during the evening.*

*Some other kids in my position might be tempted to pocket some of the money. After all, it would be pretty easy not to get caught as long as you didn't take very much. But I would never steal. First of all, everybody knows that stealing is just plain wrong. Second, that money is important to Mrs. Bray and the drama club. They need it to help pay for the costumes and the sets. If I stole from them, I would feel bad. I wouldn't be able to see myself as a good person. If I were caught stealing, I wouldn't be able to face my friends, my parents, or the rest of the school.*

*Mrs. Bray knows that I am honest and careful and that I will account for all the money accurately and turn it all in at the end of the evening.*

# Build Your Skills

**B**eing honest is something that you have to make a choice about every time you're faced with an ethical situation. However, you can learn more about the consequences of your choices in many ways.

## Education

- Study law to discover the penalties our society places on various crimes.
- Study sociology to learn about the ethical standards in various cultures around the world.
- Study history to see what impact various ethical choices have had on the world.

## Activities

- Explore the topic of honesty on the Internet. Look for sites using the search terms "business ethics" and "ethical business practices."
- Follow the news about the trial of somebody who has been dishonest. Read newspaper and online articles. Do you think the person is guilty? Why do you think he or she did this dishonest thing? What will be the consequences?
- Read a biography of a famous person and pay attention to his or her personal values. Do the person's values agree with yours?
- Read a book about famous criminals and try to figure out why some people disregard society's values entirely.

# Try It Yourself

You are working a few nights a week at the local movie theater at the candy counter. Joshua, who works with you sometimes, occasionally pockets a box of candy at the end of the evening without paying. One night you ask him about this, and he encourages you to do the same by saying, "Hey, they pay us hardly anything. They owe us a crummy box of candy anyhow."

Follow these steps to put your honesty to work:

1. Consider whether you should steal, too. Does it matter that it's only a $1.50 box of candy? Does the theater really owe you anything? You took the job for the salary they offered; is it fair to assume they owe you more?

2. Think about whether you should do anything about Joshua's stealing. Is it dishonest of you to not tell the owner that Joshua is stealing? Is it your job to report him to the theater owner or only to stay honest yourself?

Being honest on the job is difficult. You have to consider not only your actions, but also the actions of those who work with you. Not saying anything about somebody else's dishonesty may hurt your employer, but for some of us reporting on someone else's bad behavior feels wrong, too. That's why it's important that you develop your own set of values so you have the tools to face difficult ethical decisions throughout your life.

# Performance Review

**W**hat rating would an employer give you on being honest?

- Needs Improvement
- Average
- Above Average
- Outstanding

Take action to earn an Outstanding rating by doing the tasks in the following checklist.

---

### BEING HONEST CHECKLIST

- ⬭ Tell the truth.
- ⬭ Make choices that match commonly held values.
- ⬭ Make your actions consistent with your values.
- ⬭ Understand the consequences of dishonesty.
- ⬭ Always choose the ethical course of action.

---

# Words at Work

**T**hese words relate to being honest. How many can you define?

- Dishonesty
- Ethics
- Morals
- Trust
- Honor
- Sincerity
- Integrity
- Trustworthy

# PART II

## Workplace Skills

The next time you are in a store or other business, notice what the employees are doing. Most are using more than the foundation skills described in Part I. In a restaurant, for example, you may see the employees working together, serving customers, explaining information on the menu, and entering orders in a computer. These skills are called workplace skills because they are needed to do a good job.

Foundation skills help you do the basic tasks of most jobs. But employers say they need more than foundation skills from their workers. Can you think of some reasons why? Part II describes the most important workplace skills that employers want and includes suggestions for developing workplace skills now.

### Resources

You use resources to get something done. Resources can be time, money, supplies, tools, and people. Good workers know how to find, organize, and control resources. What would happen, for example, if a baker ran out of ingredients or time for baking cakes that had been ordered?

*Career Skill 17:* Managing Time

*Career Skill 18:* Managing Money

*Career Skill 19:* Managing Materials and Facilities

*Career Skill 20:* Managing People

### People Skills

Employers expect employees to work well with others. For example, employees work on teams to get a job done efficiently. Workers who are pleasant and helpful to customers keep those customers happy. What would happen to a business if the employees argued with customers and each other all day long?

*Career Skill 21:* Working in a Team

*Career Skill 22:* Teaching

*Career Skill 23:* Serving Customers

*Career Skill 24:* Leading

*Career Skill 25:* Negotiating

*Career Skill 26:* Working with Cultural Diversity

## Information

Information is everywhere! Finding and using information well helps employees make good decisions and focus on important details. Explaining information clearly helps others understand key points. What would happen, for example, if a worker took an hour to explain one simple fact to 30 coworkers?

*Career Skill 27:* Acquiring and Evaluating Information

*Career Skill 28:* Organizing and Maintaining Information

*Career Skill 29:* Interpreting and Communicating Information

*Career Skill 30:* Using Computers to Process Information

## Systems

A system is a group of items or people working together to form a unified whole with one purpose. In a business, every job and every worker affects another. A good worker understands his or her job and how it fits into the company. What would happen, for example, if one worker was careless with his or her job?

*Career Skill 31:* Understanding Systems

*Career Skill 32:* Monitoring and Correcting Performance

*Career Skill 33:* Improving and Designing Systems

## Technology

Technology can be fun and fast. Knowing how to choose and use technology on the job makes workers very effective. But what if a worker, for example, used a word-processing program to add numbers or bought expensive equipment when cheaper equipment would get the job done?

*Career Skill 34:* Selecting Technology

*Career Skill 35:* Applying Technology

*Career Skill 36:* Maintaining and Troubleshooting
Technology

# MANAGING TIME

**H**ow do you organize the time in your day or week? In school, your day is broken into organized chunks of time for each class or activity. At work nobody organizes your time for you. Are you prepared to manage your time once you're on the job?

Managing time often means juggling several types of tasks and deadlines. You have to make the right decisions about what to do first and what you can put off. Sometimes this means deciding what tasks you can skip entirely.

Managing time includes the ability to

- Select relevant, goal-related activities
- Rank activities in order of importance
- Allocate time to activities
- Understand, prepare, and follow schedules

## Careers That Use This Skill

**A**ny worker will do better by having this skill, but these careers are strongly focused on managing time:

- Project managers
- Administrative assistants
- Air traffic controllers
- Meeting planners

- Nurses
- Couriers
- Truck drivers
- Bus drivers

Young Person's Career Skills Handbook, © JIST Works

# Why Employers Want This Skill

**E**mployers pay employees for their time. How much somebody accomplishes in a workday can make the difference between a worthwhile employee and one who does not earn his paycheck. Those who run from crisis to crisis and never plan their time don't do a very good job. Those who organize their time may not finish everything; however, they seldom fail to complete the most important tasks.

Managing time involves making choices about how to spend every minute of the workday. Most jobs include several duties. For example, an administrative assistant spends some time answering phone calls, some time creating and sending out correspondence, and some time organizing meetings. Every job is different and has different responsibilities. Good time management involves understanding those responsibilities and juggling them efficiently. How effectively a person juggles the various duties of a job in the time allowed every day is an important indicator of job success.

> **"**You may delay, but time will not.**"**
> —Benjamin Franklin, statesman

# Managing Time on the Job

Name: Missy Renault

Job: Restaurant owner

*My husband Sal and I have owned the Gray Goose for 15 years. We can seat 156 people at a time, and on a busy day we have as many as 10 servers working. One of the things we take pride in is our service. Our folks are the finest food servers in the area. People know they will get fast, efficient service when they come here for lunch. Some people have only an hour to eat, and they don't want to be kept waiting.*

*When I train new servers, I emphasize that they have to know how to manage their time. A good server has to juggle five or six tables at a time. Orders have to be taken, and servers have to put together some food, like salads, and serve it. At the end of the meal, people want to get their checks, pay, and leave. Making sure all those five or six tables feel like they're getting equal attention is tricky, but servers can do it if they prioritize and set aside enough time for each task.*

*Adam is our best server. He just seems to know how to spend enough time on each table without neglecting anybody. He doesn't get bogged down in one activity and forget another. That's what we look for in a good server—one who knows the value of both our time and the customer's time.*

> **"One always has time enough if one will apply it well."**
> —Carl Friedrich Gauss, mathematician
> and astronomer

## Build Your Skills

Managing time can involve several abilities, including prioritizing, analyzing, and scheduling. You can develop this skill through your education and activities.

### Education

- Take courses in mathematics to help you learn how to calculate things, such as the amount of time you have available for various tasks or the percentage of your workday to allocate to certain tasks.

- In college you might take classes in business or project management to help you understand the various tasks that go into a workday.

- Read books or take courses in time management.

### Activities

- Set long-term goals and calculate how much time you have to make them happen. For example, if you want to learn a piece of music for a concert three months from now, how much time do you have to practice every day to become perfect?

- Use technology to help you manage your time. Computer programs such as Microsoft Outlook include a calendar function that allows you to enter tasks so you can see at a glance what activities are coming up. In addition, hand-held devices, everything from cell phones to personal digital assistants, often include scheduling programs to keep you on time when you're on the go. If you want to use a more low-tech method, buy a day planner or wall calendar.

## Try It Yourself

You have been hired as an intern at a large law firm. Your duties include answering the phone, greeting visitors, making copies as requested by legal assistants, filing, and scheduling appointments for the attorneys. How can you use good time management skills to help you handle your work?

1. Make sure you understand your priorities. For example, you probably can't delay answering the phone for very long, so the phone might be your first priority. Copying, which can be done during slow times or before the office opens for business, could be lower on your list of priorities.

2. Take advantage of slow times. Few people come into the office after 4:30 p.m., so could you take advantage of that time to do the filing?

3. Understand your deadlines. If there is a rush copy job and the phone is keeping you too busy to meet it, ask for help.

4. Create a to-do list every morning with the most important items on top. Check things off as you get to them, and try to review your list several times a day to see whether you will fit everything in. If you don't get to a lower priority task today, move it to tomorrow's list so you don't forget it.

5. Don't become distracted by tasks that aren't your responsibility. You can help others out, but don't do this so often that you fail to complete your own work.

# Performance Review

What rating would an employer give you on managing your time?

- Needs Improvement
- Average
- Above Average
- Outstanding

Take action to improve to an Outstanding rating by doing the tasks in the following checklist.

## MANAGING TIME CHECKLIST

○ List the tasks you want to accomplish for the day or week and rank them in order of importance. Make sure you complete the most important tasks.

○ Stick to the schedules you set.

○ Use tools such as day planners and scheduling software to help you manage your time.

○ Focus on your goals by scheduling time each day to work on them.

# Words at Work

These words relate to managing your time. How many can you define?

- Allocate
- Multitask
- Prioritize
- Efficiency
- Scheduling
- Commitments

# MANAGING MONEY

**W**hether you earn a six-figure annual salary or a small weekly allowance, you need to learn how to manage money. An important part of this skill is knowing how to create a budget. A budget sets boundaries for how much money you expect to make and spend. Businesses often use budgets to help them manage money.

To make a realistic budget, you have to have accurate financial information. This information includes records of earnings and expenses in the past, current costs, and future financial goals.

Managing money includes the ability to

- Use or prepare budgets
- Estimate costs and earnings
- Keep detailed records to track your budget
- Make adjustments to the budget as needed

## Careers That Use This Skill

**A**ny worker will do better by having this skill, but these careers are strongly focused on managing money:

- Accountants
  - Bookkeepers
  - Retail store managers
- Financial advisors
- Managers
- Purchasing agents

- Advertising executives
- Stock brokers
- Budget analysts
- Cost estimators
- Loan officers

# Why Employers Want This Skill

**M**any jobs involve managing how money is earned or spent. Because most companies are in business to make money, the ability to spend money wisely and keep records of your spending is important. Even if your company has a staff of accountants and bookkeepers, you may be asked to come up with a budget for your own department or project.

Although managers and supervisors are usually responsible for creating and maintaining budgets, every worker in an organization should know how the organization earns and spends money. For example, if you work in a store, you need to know which items sell the best so that you can make sure you always have those items in stock and display them so that customers can easily find them.

Employees, particularly those in management positions, are often judged on their ability to control costs and increase profits. You need to be able to use financial information to make smart money decisions. Suppose your business spent a lot of money on television commercials last month, but sales did not change. Instead of continuing to spend money on commercials, you should look for more effective ways to spend the advertising budget, such as direct mail coupons. Employees always need to consider the money involved in any decision they make.

> **"**Never spend your money before you have it.**"**
> —Thomas Jefferson, U.S. President

# Managing Money on the Job

Name: Meg Ricardo

Job: Movie producer

*I am a producer, which means that I deal with the money side of making movies. A movie can cost a lot to produce—sometimes many millions of dollars. That might seem like a lot of money, but you can use it up really fast, trust me.*

*The first day I'm assigned to a movie I start crunching numbers. I have to get budgets from various people such as the director, the costumer, the caterer, and so on. I combine all those individual budgets into one big budget for the whole movie. That's what I turn into the studio for approval.*

*When I work with people who know how to give me a good estimate of their costs and stick to it, I end up looking good at the end of the shoot. But if I work with people who don't know how to accurately create a budget and track their costs, we can come in way over budget.*

*Even though I'm dealing with millions of dollars, believe me, my bosses count every penny. I look good when I make good forecasts and keep costs down. I need people who can do the same, working for me to make it all come together.*

> **❝**Half the money I spend on advertising is wasted; the trouble is, I don't know which half. **❞**
> —**John Wanamaker, businessman**

# Build Your Skills

**M**anaging money can involve several abilities, including making forecasts, keeping records, and evaluating changes in a budget. Look for opportunities in your education and activities to develop this skill.

## Education

- Take courses in mathematics and accounting to learn how to make financial calculations.
- Learn to use computer spreadsheet programs, such as Excel or Quicken. You can use spreadsheets to create budgets or financial statements.
- Take business courses to learn about standard business financial statements and money management techniques.

## Activities

- Set up a monthly budget for yourself. For one month, record all the money you get and exactly how you spent it. Use that information as a model for your budget.
- Volunteer to help track the finances for a club or organization you belong to.
- Practice performing calculations on your calculator or computer.
- Try to save some money every month, and track what you've saved.

## Try It Yourself

You work for a publishing company that has decided to create a series of CDs based on a travel book series. They have asked you to do an initial budget for the CDs.

1. Ask questions of management to be sure you understand all about the project. How many CDs will you create and of what length? Do you have to pay the book author a fee for using the book material? What price does the company want to sell the CDs for?

2. Make a list of every type of cost you can think of, from office supplies and phone calls to recording studio time and actors to read the material.

3. Research prices so you can make a good estimate for each type of cost. Consider adding something to the total cost in case your estimates are too low; for example, add 10 percent more as a buffer in case costs come in higher.

4. Set up systems to track your actual costs against your budget. Decide whether to enter receipt amounts in a computer program or simply keep a file of receipts you can add up with a calculator.

5. Create a strategy for making adjustments to your budget as costs come in. Will you need to get management approval for costs you didn't anticipate in your budget?

Managing money means getting solid information up front about expectations, goals, and prices. As you gain experience in your business, you will make better estimates. Don't hesitate to ask those with more experience for advice when creating your first few budgets!

## Performance Review

**W**hat rating would an employer give you on managing money?

- Needs Improvement
- Average

- Above Average
- Outstanding

Take action to earn an Outstanding rating by consistently doing the tasks in the following checklist.

---

### MANAGING MONEY CHECKLIST

- ◯ Keep financial records organized and complete.
- ◯ Make a plan to save money.
- ◯ Open a savings account.
- ◯ Review your budget as you earn and spend money and make changes as necessary to keep you on track.

---

## Words at Work

**T**hese words relate to managing money. How many of them can you define?

- Forecast
- Budget
- Financial statement
- Balance sheet

- Revenue
- Cash flow
- Calculate
- Spreadsheet

# MANAGING MATERIALS AND FACILITIES

Businesses all have facilities, whether that facility is a van, kiosk, store, factory, or office. The resources of that facility, such as individual offices, furniture, and lights, have to be allocated to the people who work there. Likewise, all businesses use materials of some sort. Those materials might be office supplies, raw materials used to build things, or final products that the company sells. Workers have to make decisions about how these facilities and materials are used and handled on a daily basis.

Managing materials and facilities includes the ability to

- Acquire, store, and distribute materials, parts, and supplies
- Allocate space and equipment throughout the organization
- Set up systems to make the best use of materials and facilities

## Careers That Use This Skill

Any worker will do better by having this skill, but these careers are strongly focused on managing materials and facilities:

- Facility managers
- Office managers
- Retail store managers
- Hotel managers
  - Information technology managers
- Purchasing agents
- Dispatchers
- Electricians
- Property managers
- Chefs

# Why Employers Want This Skill

**F**acility and material resources are the main tools of business; without them work doesn't get done. Some employees, such as facility managers or office managers who order supplies, spend a lot of time planning, purchasing, and distributing resources among all employees in the company. The ability to manage these resources is key to their success and to the success of their companies.

You may not be responsible for purchasing or maintaining facilities and materials as part of your job, but all employees must use their employers' materials and facilities to do their jobs. Employers expect their employees to know how to use the equipment they are given as part of their jobs, such as a computer, and to be able to share equipment, such as copiers and printers, with other employees in a fair manner. Employers also expect employees to use materials wisely and avoid waste.

Mismanagement of facilities and materials can be costly for both employees and the employers. Chemists, for example, need to properly store and handle the chemicals they work with or they could injure themselves or others. If the night manager of a store forgets to set the alarm when he leaves, the store could be robbed. Employees who can improve the safety, security, and usefulness of the facilities they work in or the materials they work with are valuable.

> **❝**Life is constantly providing us with new funds, new resources, even when we are reduced to immobility. In life's ledger there is no such thing as frozen assets. **❞**
> —Henry Miller, **author**

# Managing Materials and Facilities on the Job

Name: Alan Mercer

Job: Operations manager for a tax preparation company

*I'm in charge of all the facilities for our company. Every year we rent offices in major cities for four months and prepare taxes for our clients. Sometimes those offices are in shopping malls, and sometimes they are in street-level office buildings. Every office has a manager who is responsible for outfitting the office with computers, supplies, and furniture.*

*The really good office managers can estimate how much of everything they will need. They look at the number of employees and estimated number of clients and calculate what they will need to operate. That makes my job a lot easier because I can place one big order for equipment and supplies and get the best price. If somebody guesses wrong, it can cost the company money to place a smaller order a few months into the work.*

*These managers are also responsible for allocating the resources. That means providing enough office space for workers and clients to meet and providing computers to the workers who need them. To get the most use out of the computers, managers sometimes have employees who work different shifts share the same computer. Allocating materials and equipment efficiently can keep costs down and employees productive in their work.*

# Build Your Skills

**Y**ou can develop your ability to manage materials and facilities through your education and activities.

### Education

- Take courses in mathematics and accounting to learn how to make financial calculations.
- Study computer software such as Visio and SmartDraw to learn how to use a computer to design spaces.
- Take business courses to learn about resource budgeting and allocation techniques.

### Activities

- Take a room in your house and measure it. Create a drawing of it on graph paper or use your computer. Now figure out how you might set up two desks in the space along with a filing cabinet and table for a printer. What is the most efficient design for two people sharing this workspace? Why?
- For two weeks, track the groceries your family uses. Create a shopping plan that would provide groceries enough for a two-week period. Keep in mind that buying groceries in bulk could save your family money!
- Track the amount of time each member of your family spends on the family computer. Figure out a schedule that allows everybody enough time to use the equipment.

# Try It Yourself

**Y**ou have been hired to set up a new office for an advertising company in a nearby city. The office space has already been rented. You need to deal with setting up the space with furniture, ordering computers and other equipment, and ordering office supplies. How could you go about it?

1. Be sure you get accurate information about the number of employees, the type of work they will be doing, and uses for the office. For example, do the employees need a place to meet with clients for conferences?

2. Allow for common areas such as a coffee and tea area or employee eating space. Could the employees use a library space for research or brainstorming projects?

3. Begin to build a budget by listing every type of resource (office supplies, furniture, computer equipment, coffee supplies, graphic design materials, and so on). Do some research online and by phone to get price estimates based on the volume of items you want to buy.

4. Determine how many supplies should be kept on hand and plan storage space appropriately. How often can you buy more supplies and still get good volume discounts? (Note that some companies give you discounts based on your annual volume, not order by order).

Managing materials and facilities involves estimating, budgeting, pricing, and distributing items to employees. Good planning is an important part of this skill!

# Performance Review

**W**hat rating would an employer give you on managing materials and facilities?

- Needs Improvement
- Average
- Above Average
- Outstanding

Take action to earn an Outstanding rating by consistently doing the tasks in the following checklist.

---

## MANAGING MATERIALS AND FACILITIES CHECKLIST

○ Learn what materials and facilities your organization needs to succeed.

○ Set up procedures to maintain facilities and organize materials.

○ Negotiate with suppliers to get materials at the best price.

○ Consider safety and security issues when dealing with materials and facilities.

---

# Words at Work

**T**hese words relate to managing materials and facilities. How many can you define?

- Allot
- Distribute
- Facility
- Adjustment
- Calculate
- Materials
- Space planning
- Replenish

# MANAGING PEOPLE

In many careers, you will have to make decisions about how to use people's time to get a job done. Managing people involves not only making choices about who will do what type of work, but also determining who has the appropriate skills for each task that's involved. You have to consider how much work each person can handle and what type of work they enjoy. In addition, you have to be able to present critical comments about a person's work in a way that will encourage improvement, not discourage that person.

Managing people includes the ability to

- Assess knowledge and skills
- Distribute work according to people's abilities
- Evaluate performance
- Provide feedback

## Careers That Use This Skill

Any worker will do better by having this skill, but these careers are strongly focused on managing people:

- Office managers
- Project managers
  - Business executives
  - Military officers
  - Factory supervisors
- Hospital administrators
- School principals
- Landscapers
- General contractors
- Interior designers

# Why Employers Want This Skill

**P**eople are an organization's most valuable resource and often the most difficult resource to manage. Part of managing people is juggling the work to be done with the number of available people and the available time. You have to make the right decisions about who has the ability to do a certain type of work.

To make the right decisions, you have to learn what skills the people you work with have, starting with yourself. When you interview for a job, you have to convince the person doing the hiring that you have the skills to do the work that the company needs you to do. When you assign work, you have to make sure each assignment fits with the person's skills. If you don't, mistakes will be made, and time will be wasted on correcting those mistakes.

Being able to give useful feedback is important, too. The best feedback is honest without being harsh. Harsh criticism from a boss or coworker can cause an employee to feel angry or sad, and these feelings rarely lead to improvement. Management may be responsible for the official employee evaluations, but a word of praise from a coworker for a job well done goes a long way toward improving an employee's attitude about the job. Likewise, listening to helpful criticism from experienced workers is often the best way to learn a job and improve job performance.

> **❝**Whatever you are by nature, keep to it; never desert your line of talent. Be what nature intended you for, and you will succeed.**❞**
> —Sydney Smith, English essayist

# Managing People on the Job

Name: Hank Pritchard

Job: Owner of a bicycle manufacturing company

*I started Cycle-Up five years ago. It was a pretty small company at first, but things have taken off in the last year or two. Last year I hired two line supervisors when I expanded my operation. Al Schenken supervises the folks who assemble the bikes. Martine Woo supervises the people who stick on the decals, polish up the fenders, and box up the bikes.*

*From day one Martine was better at figuring out work schedules. She picks the right person for each job and figures out how much work she can get out of each person every day. She lets people know if there is room for improvement and praises them if they do a good job.*

*On the other hand, Al's team is often late with work because Al underestimates how long it will take people to complete the job. Sometimes he schedules somebody who isn't as skilled to a key job, and then the whole line suffers from the bottleneck that creates. If somebody makes a mistake, Al doesn't seem to know how to help that person to improve. We've had a lot more turnover in folks who work for Al. Some even request transfers to Martine's line.*

*Knowing how to use your people to get the job done is an art. Some people just do it better than others.*

> **❝**Let each man pass his days wherein his skill is greatest. **❞**
>
> **—Sextus Propertius, Roman poet**

# Build Your Skills

You can develop your ability to manage people through your education and activities.

## Education

- Take courses in mathematics to help you learn how to calculate things, such as the amount of time it will take people to complete a task or the percentage of a person's workday to assign to various tasks.

- Read books or take courses in management to learn how to provide constructive feedback and evaluate performance.

## Activities

- Set up a daily or weekly schedule for your family's chores and see whether they can stick to it for one week. Be sure to match people's talents with the right tasks. People enjoy doing something they are good at much more than something for which they have no talent.

- Learn to use project management software such as Microsoft Project. This program enables you to enter information about workers such as their skill level, how much they get paid per hour, and availability. You can then assign those workers to individual tasks in a project.

- Use workflow diagrams to assign tasks in a project. In these diagrams, each task is written in a box, and lines connect the boxes to show the order of tasks. Write in the names of people you want to work on the tasks, making sure they aren't assigned to more than one task at a time. Create a system to rank the skill level of people, and note the level of skill that different tasks require. Be sure to match the right person with each task.

# Try It Yourself

You have been hired as the manager of a copy store. You supervise eight people who take orders, run copies, and help customers use the computers that they can rent to work on their documents.

1. Make sure you understand the various skill levels of your people. For example, who is best at using computers? Try to assign that person to deal with the computer customers as often as possible.

2. Pay attention to how quickly the employees handle certain tasks. If one person is too chatty with customers when ringing up an order, perhaps you could get more work from that person by putting her on copying projects.

3. Understand that you have to distribute the work so people get to do the things they like as well as those they dislike. Nobody likes clearing paper jams in the machines, so spread that task around so nobody has to do it all the time.

4. Create a work schedule every day to help people manage their time. List large projects and assign them to people, leaving time for dealing with customers and rush orders.

5. Give people feedback on their work on a regular basis. This feedback should include both praise and criticism. Always give criticism in a constructive way by pointing out how the person can improve and starting with a compliment about something he or she does well.

Managing people involves planning, prioritizing, assessing skills, and giving and listening to feedback. Every person is different and has different abilities. Good human resource management involves understanding those differences and using them most effectively on the job.

# Performance Review

What rating would an employer give you on managing people?

- Needs Improvement
- Average
- Above Average
- Outstanding

Take action to earn an Outstanding rating by consistently doing the tasks in the following checklist.

---

## MANAGING PEOPLE CHECKLIST

○ Give people positive feedback when they do something well.

○ Know the skills of the people you work with, including yourself.

○ Match the person to the task as much as you can.

○ Be kind and honest when you criticize someone's work.

---

# Words at Work

These words relate to managing people. How many can you define?

- Proficiency
- Human resources
- Tact
- Feedback
- Evaluate
- Assign
- Project management
- Assess

# WORKING IN A TEAM

**A** team is any group of people that comes together to accomplish something. For example, a basketball team works together to win games. Working on a team involves getting along with other people, as well as doing your share of the work. You have to be able to communicate with other people and work through differences in order to achieve the goal.

Working on a team includes the ability to

- Contribute ideas and effort
- Do your share of the work
- Encourage team members
- Resolve differences

## Careers That Use This Skill

**A**ny worker will do better by having this skill, but these careers directly involve working with a team:

- Coaches
- Project managers
- Directors
- Firefighters
- Musicians

- Nurses
- Construction workers
- Assembly line workers
- Urban planners

# Why Employers Want This Skill

In the workplace, many projects require teams of people to be successful. That's because a variety of talents and experience are needed to accomplish many tasks. For this reason, the ability to work well as a member of a team is useful in many jobs.

Employers often refer to the ability to work well as a member of a team as being a "team player." Team players always do their part and work for the good of the team, not just themselves. Team players respect the other members of the team and know that each team member has something to contribute. They feel a sense of responsibility that goes beyond the piece of the project they are assigned. They communicate with the other team members to make sure everyone is working toward the goal. Teams that include good team players tend to achieve their goals, so their employers are therefore more successful.

People who are not team players want to do everything their own way and don't listen to suggestions and ideas from other team members. They are eager to highlight their personal accomplishments when a project succeeds and to point fingers at other team members when it fails. They tend to cause conflicts instead of solve problems. The behavior of these people often keeps their teams from reaching their goals. As a result, their employers are less successful.

> **"**The important thing to recognize is that it takes a team, and the team ought to get credit for the wins and the losses. **"**
>
> —Phillip Caldwell, Ford Motor Company executive

# Working in a Team on the Job

Name: Callie Reynolds

Job: Marketing manager for a greeting card company

*Last month my boss asked me to organize a marketing campaign for a new line of greeting cards. A marketing campaign involves creating promotional materials such as press kits, advertisements, and brochures. No one person can do all this work, so I met with Rick, Jan, Peter, and Antonio to figure out how we could work as a team to complete the campaign.*

*Rick is a writer, so he was going to write all the ads and a brochure. Jan is a graphic designer; her job was to design the ads and brochures. Antonio's experience is in public relations, so he was assigned to put together the press kits. Peter is with our accounting department. He was going to help me create a budget for the campaign and assemble quotes from various printers.*

*From the beginning, some people worked better on the team than others. For example, Jan didn't communicate with the rest of the team about her progress. At one of the weekly team meetings, I discovered she was behind in her work on the brochure, which put the project in trouble. Peter, on the other hand, was unwilling to change his ideas of how things should be done, so he often argued with other team members.*

*Antonio and Rick were better team players. Antonio communicated very well with the other team members and asked for help when he needed it. Rick was willing to do the extra work to help out Antonio with the press kits. No team is perfect, but people who know how to work well with others are valuable to a manager like me.*

# Build Your Skills

**E**xperience in dealing with people is one of the best ways to get better at working with them. Take advantage of any opportunities you have to work as part of a team.

## Education

- Take a speech or drama class to improve your communication skills.
- Take classes in psychology or sociology to understand how people think and work together.

## Activities

- Join a sports team. Notice how it takes the contribution of all the members, not just a star player, to win.
- Participate in an activity that involves working with other people to produce something, such as acting in a play or playing a musical instrument in a band.
- Notice how your family works as a team. Does everybody contribute equally? Is your family good at resolving differences? What could your family members do to become a better team?
- The next time you need help to get a job done, assemble a team of people to work with you. Make sure everybody understands his or her job and find ways to help them communicate about their progress.

> **"**Teamwork is no accident. It is the byproduct of good leadership.**"**
>
> —John Adair, authority on leadership

# Try It Yourself

**Y**ou work in a factory making DVD players on the assembly line. Your boss asks you to be part of a committee made up of workers and managers. The committee's job is to come up with a new safety handbook for new workers. What can you do to be a good member of this team?

1. Make sure you understand what your responsibilities are. Ask questions if you need to.

2. Do the work that is expected of you and meet any deadlines you are given. If you are having difficulty with the work or think that you won't meet a deadline, talk with the team leader as soon as possible. That way the leader can help you solve the problem and keep the project on track.

3. Talk with the other team members on a regular basis. Keep them posted on your progress and stay aware of their activities in case they need help. Be encouraging. If you think another team member has done a good job with his part of the handbook, tell him so.

4. If you run into a misunderstanding or problem with another team member, find positive ways to work through the situation and resolve it. Think about the things you and the other person have in common, and keep the focus on the goal instead of personal differences.

5. Contribute ideas and suggestions that will be helpful to the team. Make sure you present any criticism you have in a constructive way. Your criticism should explain how to improve, not just point blame.

# Performance Review

**W**hat rating would an employer give you on working in a team?

- Needs Improvement
- Average
- Above Average
- Outstanding

Take action to earn an Outstanding rating by consistently doing the tasks in the following checklist.

---

## WORKING IN A TEAM CHECKLIST

○ Know what tasks you are responsible for; do them well and complete them on time.

○ Do whatever you can to help the team accomplish its goal.

○ Speak up when you see a problem, but make sure you can also offer a solution.

○ Motivate your team by providing encouragement and having a positive attitude.

---

# Words at Work

**T**hese words relate to working in a team. How many can you define?

- Participate
- Communicate
- Constructive
- Cooperate
- Contribute
- Resolve
- Expectations
- Responsibility
- Conflict

# TEACHING

**A**ll of us are teachers in some way. Maybe you helped your younger brother learn how to tie his shoelaces, or perhaps you taught your friends a song. In the working world, you will be asked to teach others frequently, whether you hold a formal teaching position or you simply help a new employee to learn the ropes. When you teach someone, you communicate information in a way that the person understands.

Teaching includes the ability to

- Identify important information and organize it so the learner can understand it
- Communicate effectively with others
- Use tools such as visual aids or specific examples to make your point
- Respond to questions

## Careers That Use This Skill

**A**ny worker will do better by having this skill, but these careers directly involve teaching others:

- Teachers
- College professors
- Computer support specialists
- Corporate trainers
- Dog trainers
- Health educators
- Fitness workers
- Managers
- Coaches

## Why Employers Want This Skill

**W**hen you are doing a job, you learn a lot of details. You learn procedures and terms. You know how to deal with various situations, how to fill out certain forms, and so on. The ability to teach that knowledge is valuable to employers because with this ability you can help those you work with do a better job.

Teaching employees is a major expense for most employers. Employers have to either hire special trainers or take experienced workers away from their regular jobs to teach new employees. Employees who are not taught their jobs well make more mistakes and take a longer time to become productive. Employees who are taught well make fewer mistakes and take a shorter amount of time to work up to speed.

Good teachers are able to communicate effectively. Communication involves one person providing information and another person receiving that information and processing it. An important part of effective communication is making sure that the person you are talking to understands what you are saying. Part of the learning process is also making sure that the person remembers what you taught. In the modern workplace where things are continually changing, the transfer of knowledge has become even more important, and teaching has become an even more valued skill.

# Teaching on the Job

Name: Marcus Wolokosky

Job: Training manager for a Web-based gift basket store

*The Gift Basket is an Internet store that sells baskets of candy, cookies, and fruit. When the holiday rush hits, the store is really busy, and management has to hire lots of new people to assemble baskets and fill orders.*

*When I started here as training manager five years ago, I noticed that the people in the training department used to go crazy this time of year. They had a training program in place, but because the trainers didn't really know the job they were teaching, the new workers made a lot of mistakes when they got to the shop floor. The trainer had trouble handling both the computer software training classes for office staff and the sales skills classes for the salespeople.*

*In response to this problem, I started a mentoring program. Each new employee worked alongside the experienced worker who was assigned to be his or her mentor. First the new person watched how the mentor did the work. Then the new person did the work, and the mentor gave feedback. It worked great, most of the time. Of course, some people were better at training new people than others.*

*Having good mentors has become so important that the managers look for teaching ability when they hire new assemblers. It's not a job requirement exactly, but they try to get enough people who are good at communicating information to keep the mentoring program going. It saves the company a lot of time and money, believe me!*

# Build Your Skills

You can develop this skill through your education and activities.

## Education

- For one day, observe your teachers in class. What did the most effective teachers do to help people learn? What didn't work as well?

- Take courses in writing and speech to improve your communication skills.

- Take classes in psychology to understand how people learn.

- Take education courses in college to learn methods for teaching effectively.

## Activities

- Offer to teach friends something you're good at, such as chess, reading music, or astronomy.

- Volunteer to give a talk to a class or club made up of younger children on a topic you are familiar with.

- Read books to discover theories of how people learn. Some people are visual learners, for example; that means they need to see something to be able to understand it. Others learn by associating ideas. Try to figure out how you learn.

# Try It Yourself

You have been working in the mailroom of a large corporation for a year. You have been studying computer science at the local college at night and have just been promoted to the technical support department. You have been asked to train your replacement in the mailroom. How would you go about teaching this other person your job?

1. Sit down and make a list of the things you do every day. You probably do more than you think.

2. Determine the right sequence for teaching the new employee. Are there simpler tasks you should teach first? Should you just take the person through a typical workday? What order of information could the person absorb most easily?

3. Figure out what tools are available that could help you teach your replacement. Has the company developed procedures checklists or diagrams that would help this person learn your job? If not, could you develop these tools on your own?

4. As you teach your replacement, ask the person frequently if you are going too fast or if you should go over something one more time. People can easily become overwhelmed with a lot of new information.

5. Answer questions as they come up. If you don't know the answer, get the answer and be sure to follow up. Encourage the person you are teaching to take notes so he or she can refer to them later when you've left for your new position.

6. Give the person your contact information so he or she can call you for help after you change jobs. Many questions won't come up until the person has been working on the job for several weeks.

## Performance Review

**W**hat rating would an employer give you on teaching?

- Needs Improvement
- Average
- Above Average
- Outstanding

Take action to earn an Outstanding rating by consistently doing the tasks in the following checklist.

---

### TEACHING CHECKLIST

○ Present information in a logical order.

○ Repeat important information several times. Repetition helps people retain information.

○ Ask the person you're teaching to repeat what you've said in his or her own words to show that he or she has understood your meaning.

○ Encourage questions. Questions are a great way to clarify what's being said and receive additional information.

---

## Words at Work

**T**hese words relate to teaching. How many can you define?

- Training
- Communicate
- Mentor
- Tutor
- Learning theory
- Illustration
- Clarify
- Retain

# SERVING CUSTOMERS

**I**n most careers you deal with customers. Sometimes those customers are people who buy your company's product or service. In other cases, your customers are the people inside your company who you help. For example, you might help other employees understand their insurance benefits. Customers usually are what keep a business going, so being able to serve them well is an important skill for everybody to have, from the mail clerk to the company president.

Serving customers includes the ability to

- Be helpful
- Communicate effectively
- Handle conflicts calmly
- Satisfy customer expectations

## Careers That Use This Skill

**A**ny worker will do better by having this skill, but these careers are strongly focused on serving customers:

- Retail store clerks
- Customer service representatives
  - Salespeople
  - Flight attendants
- Hotel clerks

- Food servers
- Travel agents
- Recreation workers
- Bank tellers
- Auto repairers
- Hairstylists

# Why Employers Want This Skill

**S**erving customers well means providing the service or product the customer wants in a timely and professional way. When you are serving customers, you are representing your employer, and it's important that you interact with the customer in a positive, professional way.

Customers who do not receive the service they expect from a business often stop buying services or products from that business. They also tell everyone they know about their negative experience. This criticism can cause the business to lose sales. Customers may also complain to the manager about the bad service they received. Managers often fire employees who receive several customer complaints.

Ideally, you are always able to give customers exactly what they want. But the true test of customer service skills happens when things go wrong, and a delay or problem occurs. In that case, you have to be honest with the customer, admit the problem, and correct it as soon as possible. This task can be tough when somebody is upset at you, especially if you have no control over the situation. People who serve customers well are able to calm angry customers and find a way to satisfy them.

Serving customers well is a key to career success. If, for example, you are a food server who provides excellent customer service, you are likely to receive higher tips. Customers who are pleased with the service you provide may tell your manager, and nothing impresses a manager more than praise from customers.

# Serving Customers on the Job

Name: Martine Berger

Job: Office manager for an auto repair shop

*When folks come into Hurry Up Auto Mechanics, they're usually in a hurry. They have a problem with their car, and they want it fixed as soon as possible. I'm the one who sits at the front desk and writes up the service order when the customers come in and the one they pay when the car's all fixed up.*

*Most of the time these folks deal with me, but when the job is done, a mechanic comes out with their keys and explains to them what was wrong with the car and how it was fixed. Some of the mechanics are good at dealing with people, and some...well, let's just say they're good at fiddling with an engine, but when it comes to people, they have a lot to learn.*

*Take Sandy and Pete, for instance. Sandy hates talking to customers. She's real nervous around people and never says things like please and thank you. She doesn't take the time to explain the work that was done, not even when the work ends up being more involved and expensive than the customers expected. She just rushes them out. Pete, on the other hand, always greets people in a friendly way. He explains clearly what work went on and why it was needed. People always leave feeling they got a good deal and a job well done when they talk to Pete.*

*Guess you wouldn't think an auto mechanic needs good customer skills, what with working on engines all day. But when a promotion comes up for shop supervisor, I just know it's going to be Pete who gets it.*

# Build Your Skills

Take advantage of opportunities in your education and activities to develop your customer service skills.

## Education

- Take courses in writing and speech to improve your communication skills.

- Take classes in psychology or sociology to understand how people think.

- Take business courses to understand the role of customers in a successful business.

## Activities

- Take a part-time job in a retail store.

- Observe how people in stores, doctor's offices, and other places of business deal with customers. Notice what kind of attitude works best when dealing with people.

- Research successful companies online and try to figure out the role good customer service plays in their success.

- For one day, think of your teachers as your customers; after all, they expect something from you, such as homework or participation in class. Do the best you can to make your customers happy. How did this affect your relationship to your teachers? How did it feel?

> **"**Your most unhappy customers are your greatest source of learning. **"**
>
> —Bill Gates, chairman and founder of Microsoft Corporation

# Try It Yourself

**Y**ou are working as a cashier in a local market on a busy Saturday morning. One customer writes a check, but it doesn't clear your system. You ask the customer if she can pay another way. She insists you run the check through again, which you do. By now the four other people in line behind her are getting upset at the delay. What could you do to take good care of all your customers?

1. Don't forget to take care of the person in front of you, even though you are aware of the people waiting behind. The person causing the delay may be embarrassed by the situation. All the people waiting may be in this situation someday and would expect you to be polite and professional with them.

2. Talk to the people who are waiting to tell them that there's a short delay, but that you will get to them as quickly as possible.

3. Tell your customers that you understand their frustration. Don't leave them in the dark; help them to see that you're doing your best to move things forward.

4. Ask your manager or coworkers for help to resolve the issue. This delay reflects on your store, not just on you, and your manager should be eager to help out. Perhaps he can shift some of the waiting customers to another checkout line.

5. Don't forget to use humor and simply talk to the people waiting in a friendly manner. They are all people, and they can sympathize with the pressure you are under. People are often willing to help each other if they understand the situation and don't feel ignored.

# Performance Review

**W**hat rating would an employer give you on serving customers?

- Needs Improvement
- Average
- Above Average
- Outstanding

Take action to earn an Outstanding rating by consistently doing the tasks in the following checklist.

---

## SERVING CUSTOMERS CHECKLIST

- ◯ Be polite and friendly, even if you're rushed.

- ◯ Do your best to fulfill the customer's expectations. If you can't, explain why and offer some other option to make it up to him or her.

- ◯ Show that you understand the customer's point of view.

- ◯ Admit when a situation is frustrating for the customer and work hard to make things right.

---

# Words at Work

**T**hese words relate to serving customers. How many can you define?

- Customer service
- Client
- Expectations
- Satisfy
- Gratuity
- Polite
- Frustration
- Attitude

# LEADING

Leading is more than just being in charge. Leadership involves the ability to communicate your ideas or passion to others, to provide a vision, and to motivate people to act. A leader often takes a group in a new, bold direction, challenging the way things are in a responsible way. Whether you are leading an entire country or a person assigned to work on a project with you, you need the same basic set of leadership skills.

Leading includes the ability to

- Communicate thoughts, feelings, and ideas
- Provide your vision of a goal
- Encourage, persuade, and motivate people or groups
- Responsibly challenge existing procedures or authority

## Careers That Use This Skill

Any worker will do better by having this skill, but these careers are strongly focused on leading:

- Business executives
- Military officers
- Politicians
- Wilderness guides
- Ship captains
- School principals
- Lodging managers
- Construction managers

# Why Employers Want This Skill

The world is always changing. In order to continue being successful, organizations must change as well, and they count on leaders to help them do that. For this reason, employers are always looking for people who have the necessary skills to develop into leaders.

Leaders make things happen. They have solid ideas about how to improve their organizations and have the confidence and people skills to convince others to go along with their ideas. Strong leaders can attract other talented employees by creating a positive, productive work environment where employees feel valued. In contrast, managers with poor leadership skills can cause good employees to leave organizations by making the employees feel disrespected, underappreciated, or overworked. If investors or customers feel a leader is taking a company in a bad direction, they might stop doing business with that company.

Leaders are responsible for the success or failure of the groups they lead. When leaders make big changes, they risk losing their jobs if the changes turn out badly. But with this risk and responsibility comes the possibility of great rewards. Leaders often earn more money than other workers and take pride in knowing that they help shape the organizations they work for.

> **"**Progress occurs when courageous, skillful leaders seize the opportunity to change things for the better.**"**
> —Harry S Truman, U.S. President

# Leading on the Job

Name: Annette Richards

Job: Vice president of human resources for a music box manufacturer

*Musical Lights manufactures fine music boxes. It has offices in three different countries and sells its boxes all over the world, as well as on the Internet. When the company has a job opening for a high-level executive, I oversee the interview process.*

*The first thing I look for in anybody who will manage a process or other people is leadership. People who can communicate their vision and get others excited about it are the ones who help to make the company grow. They are willing to think outside of the box and try new things. When you have a great leader, the morale of the people working with that person is always higher.*

*When I interview for positions where I think leadership is especially important, I pose challenging questions. For example, I might ask what the person would do if he or she were assigned to run a department where morale was low. A good leader might say that she would provide new goals, communicate with the employees about their importance, and motivate them to be part of the team, for example.*

*Good leaders hold a company together and move it forward. Once the company had a manager of the manufacturing group who knew music boxes inside and out. He knew all about streamlined manufacturing techniques and how to get a good price for parts. But he was not a good leader. He didn't communicate well with people, and in the end he failed. Without good leadership, people don't enjoy their work or understand why they're doing what they're doing, and that situation just about guarantees failure.*

# Build Your Skills

You can learn to lead by taking advantage of opportunities in your education and extracurricular activities.

## Education

- Take a class in speech to learn how to communicate persuasively.
- Study psychology to understand what motivates people.
- In history class, pay special attention to the actions of leaders throughout time. Learn from their successes and their mistakes.

## Activities

- Run for office in your school's student council or another school club or community organization to which you belong. The campaign will provide plenty of opportunities for you to communicate your vision and practice your persuasive speaking. If you are elected, you can put your plans into action.
- Volunteer to lead an activity, project, or team. Look for ways to motivate people toward a common goal.
- Browse the business section of your local library or bookstore for books on leadership. Often these books are written by current business leaders and are filled with real-world stories that illustrate what works. You should also read a few biographies of great leaders. Notice what these leaders have in common, and in what ways they differ.

> **"**Leadership is based on inspiration, not domination; on cooperation, not intimidation.**"**
> —William Arthur Wood, author

## Try It Yourself

**R**ecognizing the procedures or established systems that are holding an organization back from change is part of leadership. Once a leader recognizes what isn't working well, he or she has to replace it with something that does. Then the leader has to explain the benefits of the new way of doing things and motivate people to do it.

Suppose you are put in charge of the annual candy sale to raise money for the school band. How can you make the most of this leadership opportunity?

1. Look at the current situation and evaluate its success. What methods does the band currently use to sell candy? Does the band need more money this year to meet higher expenses? Have sales gone down, remained the same, or improved over the past few years?

2. Try to imagine whether you could improve the situation with change. If sales have stayed the same every year, could you improve on those sales? Do you need to? If sales have gone down, there is a more urgent need to improve sales.

3. Look at your competitors. If other schools in your city are improving sales while yours are falling off, there may be a way to change how you're doing things that will improve the situation.

4. Analyze the risk of change. If your sales are good, change could cause them to drop. If your sales are poor, what do you have to lose by trying a new approach?

## Performance Review

What rating would an employer give you on leading?

- Needs Improvement
- Average

- Above Average
- Outstanding

Take action to earn an Outstanding rating by consistently doing the tasks in the following checklist.

---

### LEADING CHECKLIST

○ Find out as much as you can about the group you are leading. Use this information to help you find ways to improve on what the group is doing.

○ Involve the group in setting its own goals.

○ Be enthusiastic about your approach to the group's goals. Your enthusiasm will help to motivate the group.

○ Recognize the contribution of everybody in the group.

---

## Words at Work

These words relate to leading. How many can you define?

- Control
- Guidance
- Direct
- Management

- Status quo
- Persuasive
- Motivate
- Facilitate

# NEGOTIATING

**B**ecause people have different experiences, expectations, and personalities, they have to find ways to come to an agreement whenever they work together. The process of working out an agreement is called negotiating. People who are skilled in this process are very helpful in the workplace. They find ways for people to compromise or come up with a solution that works for everybody.

Negotiating includes the ability to

- Identify common goals
- Clearly present your position
- Understand the other person's position
- Examine possible options
- Make compromises

## Careers That Use This Skill

**A**ny worker will do better by having this skill, but these careers are strongly focused on negotiating:

- Judges
- Social workers
  - Police
  - Politicians
  - Psychologists
- Purchasing agents
- Buyers
- Attorneys
- Real estate agents

# Why Employers Want This Skill

In order to grow, organizations need to be able to make deals with other organizations. For example, a community nonprofit organization might make an agreement with the local school system to provide after-school care in the school buildings. To make these agreements, they need employees who can make deals that achieve their organization's goals.

People who work with laws, such as lawyers or police, often have to negotiate agreements between people who are very angry. These negotiators must do their best to keep everyone calm and focused on reaching an agreement. Skilled negotiators can prevent workers from going on strike or stop countries from going to war.

Negotiating may involve simply getting people to agree, but often negotiating is focused on money. Buyers and purchasing agents, for example, spend most of their time on the job negotiating the best prices on materials and services from suppliers. Good negotiators save their employers money on everything from computers to coffee filters.

Negotiating successfully usually involves being well prepared. You have to know what the current situation is, and you need to research any related facts and figures. When you have strong negotiating skills, you can help yourself, as well as your employer. You can negotiate for a higher salary or flexible hours, for example.

> **"**A compromise is the art of dividing a cake in such a way that everyone believes he has the biggest piece.**"**
> —Ludwig Erhard, German Chancellor

# Negotiating on the Job

Name: Terrence Peterson

Job: Supervisor at an ice cream production plant

*I've been a supervisor here at Really Fine Ice Cream for 10 years. Not a day goes by that I don't have to find ways to help people come to agreement about something. One guy thinks he knows the best way to do something, but another guy thinks he knows better. Or I have to get a supplier to come down in price so that I can stick to my budget.*

*I hired this new line manager, Mary Hill, a few months ago. Mary has a knack for negotiating with people. She calms everybody down and points out the things they have in common. Then she helps them look at the facts and come to an agreement about the right thing to do.*

*Workers like Mary are a gift. They keep things moving and look for solutions that make everybody happy. Mary communicates well with people and is able to get people to meet her halfway. Mary is going places because no matter what her job is, she knows how to negotiate successfully with coworkers, suppliers, and even customers.*

> **❝**Let us never negotiate out of fear.... But let us never fear to negotiate. **❞**
> —**John F. Kennedy, U.S. President**

# Build Your Skills

You can develop your negotiating skills through your education and activities.

### Education

- Take a speech class to learn persuasive speaking. In language arts, focus on learning to write persuasively.

- When you learn about treaties and other important political agreements in history class, think about the negotiation that was necessary. What were the goals of the people involved? Was the compromise a success?

### Activities

- Try negotiating with your parents. Your goal might be a bigger allowance, a pet, or a party. Think about what your parents' concerns might be and have facts ready to answer them. Also, have options in mind so that you can work out a compromise. For example, they might agree to a sleepover with a few friends instead of a big party. Remember to remain calm; whining and yelling are not the best way to negotiate. You might be surprised at your results!

- Practice negotiating prices at a garage sale or swap meet. Before you start talking, have a price in mind. (Look on the Internet to figure out what a reasonable price is.) Be prepared to walk away if the person you are dealing with doesn't come close to the price you want.

# Try It Yourself

**Y**ou have just started work as the office manager for a small insurance office. One of your jobs is to buy office supplies. There are two office supply stores in town. The person who was in your job before usually used the more expensive store because it delivered supplies more quickly. Although your boss likes the quick delivery time, she also has asked you to get the best price you can on supplies. What can you do to negotiate a better price?

1. Try to understand the situation by studying both supplier catalogues to verify how much more various items cost. Add up how much your company spends on supplies every year.

2. Check how often the former office manager ordered supplies. If you ordered more frequently, could you live with a longer delivery time?

3. Look at any other possible options, such as ordering supplies online. You might try placing a small online order to see how quickly you receive the supplies.

4. Now that you understand the situation and your options, call the less expensive store and ask whether it can deliver supplies more quickly.

5. Call the more expensive store and ask whether it would give you a discount based on the volume of supplies you order every year.

6. Make sure each store understands that if it can't help you with delivery times or price, you may take your business to the other store. Don't threaten; just be clear about your situation and what you see as your options.

7. Make your decision.

## Performance Review

What rating would an employer give you on negotiating?

- Needs Improvement
- Average
- Above Average
- Outstanding

Take action to earn an Outstanding rating by consistently doing the tasks in the following checklist.

---

### NEGOTIATING CHECKLIST

◯ Before you speak with anybody, educate yourself about the situation and know the result you want.

◯ Have more than one option available. If your options are limited, you have less room for negotiation.

◯ Be clear about your goals and options in discussions and be professional when you ask for something.

---

## Words at Work

These words relate to negotiating. How many can you define?

- Arbitrator
- Mediator
- Bargain
- Settle
- Contract
- Compromise
- Pact
- Dispute

# WORKING WITH CULTURAL DIVERSITY

**A** culture is what you grow up with and includes everything from the language people in your family or town speak to acceptable table manners, the music you listen to, the education you received, and the way you do your work. People who come from different backgrounds or different parts of the country or the world often do not do things the same way. Everybody has different experiences. The word *diversity* relates to differences among individuals in a group.

Working with cultural diversity includes the ability to

- Work well with people of different backgrounds
- Understand and appreciate cultural differences
- Help people make cultural adjustments

## Careers That Use This Skill

**A**ny worker will do better by having this skill, but people in these careers often work with people from many different cultures:

- Social workers
- Teachers
- Airline employees
- Travel agents
- Translators
- Human resources managers
- Custom agents
- Police

# Why Employers Want This Skill

Cultural diversity in many workplaces is a reality; learning and benefiting from it is better than being frustrated by it. Diversity on the job can make for a more interesting workplace. Different perspectives on a problem can result in a more creative solution.

On the other hand, culture clashes can make communication difficult and keep people from reaching their goals. Some people make the mistake of assuming that everybody thinks like they do instead of asking others how they usually approach things. People need to reach out to others to overcome differences that are interfering with working together successfully. For example, if somebody does something that bothers you, ask that person why he or she does that. Understanding this may help you get comfortable with their style. Be willing to explain why you do things a certain way and make sure others are comfortable with you.

Nearly every employer is affected by the global economy and has to work with other cultures as employees, suppliers, or customers. Employees who are comfortable working with cultural diversity can help people overcome prejudice and see each other as people. Employees with this skill are valuable because they help create a more positive, friendly, and productive work environment.

> **"**Diversity is the one true thing we all have in common. Celebrate it everyday.**"**
> **—Anonymous**

# Working with Cultural Diversity on the Job

Name: Rwanda Imbibi

Job: Video store manager

*Movie Mania is a small retail store with few employees, so it's important that all the employees get along with each other. After all, they have to work together every day to make our customers happy. Even though this is a medium-sized city, the people who live here come from all over the world and from different ethnic backgrounds. When I hire somebody, I try to make sure they will work well with others who are different from them.*

*The other day, for example, Rudy, who is from a small town in Iowa, was late getting to work. I knew from talking to him that in Rudy's laid-back small town, people aren't so exact about schedules. His small-town background has also given him an easygoing, friendly manner, and customers like him. Jamaica, who is from New York City, grew up in a fast-paced world and is always on time for everything. She takes less time with each customer, but she does a lot of work. As a manager, I like the balance of treating customers well and keeping things moving that I get when these two work together.*

*Jamaica made a comment about Rudy's lateness the other week. I pointed out that he always stays late or takes a shorter lunch to make up for occasionally being late. I asked Jamaica to be more tolerant of Rudy's style, and I asked Rudy to try to be on time. I explained to him that promptness is important to Jamaica and me. I won't change either of them completely, but I think they've both learned something about how to compromise and work with each other's differences to get the job done.*

# Build Your Skills

Look for opportunities in your education and activities to develop your ability to work with cultural diversity.

## Education

- Study another language. The way other cultures speak is sometimes a clue to how they think.

- In social studies class, learn as much as you can about other cultures. Start by learning the basics of world geography and reading about major current world events.

## Activities

- Attend a cultural festival. Many communities host festivals throughout the summer and fall to celebrate people's different national heritages. These festivals offer food, music, dancing, and people who can answer your questions about different cultures in your community.

- Go beyond pizza and tacos and try some Thai, German, Greek, or other ethnic food. Food is a fun way to learn about other cultures. (If you pick an Asian restaurant, practice eating with chopsticks!) Most ethnic restaurants offer a sampler platter so that you can taste a lot of different things. If you're not sure about something, ask your server for advice.

- Whenever you can, travel to other places; observe how people think and act in that culture.

# Try It Yourself

**Y**ou work in the shipping department of a stereo equipment manufacturer and are part of a committee to help workers resolve differences. One day Helen approaches you and says that she wants to talk to the committee about Layla, a woman who has just began working for the company as a customer service agent. Layla is Muslim and takes breaks twice a day to pray. (Muslims must pray five times a day according to the Islamic religion.) Helen and other employees feel resentful that the company allows her to take these breaks. How would you and the committee resolve this?

1. Try to find common ground. Layla may take short breaks to pray, but do others in the company take equal breaks to drink coffee, check on their child's day care, or take medicine? Can you show the benefit of each worker in the company being given some consideration for their needs and culture?

2. Find out if there are other issues bothering Helen and others. Is there something about Layla that bothers them, but they are using this cultural difference as an excuse?

3. Look at practical options. If Layla were on a different schedule, could she take fewer prayer breaks?

4. Get everybody talking. Sometimes the key to working out cultural diversity issues is to help everybody understand everybody else's position.

5. Beyond asking people to tolerate each other, ask people to celebrate their differences. Hold a potluck lunch with everybody bringing different ethnic dishes to share. Have one employee mentor a foreign employee in English in exchange for help learning the foreign language.

# Performance Review

**W**hat rating would an employer give you on working with cultural diversity?

- Needs Improvement
- Average

- Above Average
- Outstanding

Take action to earn an Outstanding rating by consistently doing the tasks in the following checklist.

## WORKING WITH CULTURAL DIVERSITY CHECKLIST

- ◯ Avoid making assumptions about people.
- ◯ Work to improve communication and increase understanding.
- ◯ Focus on common goals instead of different ways of working.

# Words at Work

**T**hese words relate to working with cultural diversity. How many can you define?

- Culture
- Diversity
- Ethnic
- Heritage

- Immigrant
- Stereotype
- Prejudice
- Custom

# ACQUIRING AND EVALUATING INFORMATION

**W**hen was the last time you needed information to accomplish something? It probably wasn't more than a day or two ago—or even an hour or two ago! Acquiring information might involve looking it up in a book or on the Internet, or it might require that you compile the information from different sources. When you find the information, you must evaluate whether it is what you need and whether it is current and accurate.

The skill of acquiring and evaluating information includes the ability to

- Identify the need for data
- Collect data from existing sources or create it
- Evaluate the relevance and accuracy of information

## Careers That Use This Skill

**A**ny worker will do better by having this skill, but people in these careers are often required to acquire and evaluate information:

- Researchers
- Private investigators
  - Paralegals
  - Journalists
- Insurance adjusters
- Police detectives
- Market researchers
- Scientists
- Engineers
- Computer programmers
- Mechanics
- Repairers

## Why Employers Want This Skill

Most businesses need information to survive. They need information about their customers such as names, addresses, and order history. They use information about their competitors to make decisions about their future. Because businesses count on information to function, the ability to acquire and evaluate information is an important skill for employees to have.

When you first start on a job, finding information can be quite a challenge. Although most employers will train you on how to use their specific systems, they will expect you to already know how to use computers to do basic research such as searching for information in a database or finding information on the Internet. Often you will have to gather information from other people on the job as well. It takes time to learn which people on the job are reliable sources of information.

Employers also count on employees to judge which information is relevant and which is irrelevant. Deciding which information is relevant involves knowing something about the topic, who the information is for, and how those people will use the information. As an employee, you may be asked to prepare presentations, write reports, or answer questions about the work that you do. Your managers will expect you to give them the information they need to make good decisions without wasting their time with unnecessary detail or unrelated topics.

> **"** Knowledge is of two kinds. We know a subject ourselves, or we know where we can find information on it. **"**
>
> —Samuel Johnson, author

# Acquiring and Evaluating Information on the Job

Name: Melissa Kraynak

Job: Customer service manager for an online electronics store

*When customers call the customer service department for the Robot World Online Electronics Store, they typically need help. Perhaps an order hasn't arrived on time, or maybe there's a problem with the billing to their credit cards. They might be having a problem locating a specific product on our Web site. The customer service representatives are responsible for making sure customers get the help they need.*

*Customer service representatives need two things to do well at this job: a friendly, polite manner and the ability to find and use information. They might have to go into the computer and find a copy of the customer's order, for example. Or they may have to ask a customer the right questions to understand the situation. If they are asked whether Robot World carries a certain type of product, they have to locate the correct catalog and figure out which product might meet the customer's needs.*

*Not everybody can locate the right information for each customer request. Some take longer finding it or find the wrong information. That takes a lot of time, and in customer service, time is money. You spend too much time with one customer, and another one is sitting on hold getting angrier by the second. If the customers are really angry or dissatisfied, they ask for me. If I find out that the customer was treated rudely or given the wrong information, I make sure the customer service person who was involved knows he or she messed up, that's for sure. After all, if we can't keep the customers happy, Robot World won't be in business too long.*

# Build Your Skills

Look for opportunities in your education and activities to develop your ability to acquire and evaluate information.

### Education

- Take courses in computers to learn how to use the Internet, search engines, and browser software. Learn how to come up with search terms that return relevant information.

- Familiarize yourself with your school library and its systems so you know how to research a topic in print.

- Take a course in journalism or work for the school paper to practice doing research and interviewing people.

### Activities

- When you are doing research for a school project, think of as many sources of information about the topic as you can. Some sources are up-to-date and accurate; others are not updated that often. Check the date the publication or Web site was last updated. Some sources include opinions, but not necessarily facts. Others include facts only. Opinions may or may not be accurate, though they can be thought provoking. Which are you looking for? Find the right source for your needs.

- Try different search engines on the Internet; each searches in a slightly different way and returns a different set of results. Be sure you spell words correctly and look for the appropriate form of a word.

# Try It Yourself

**Y**ou are a paralegal in a large law firm. One of the lawyers has asked you to research the background of a defendant charged with embezzlement (stealing money from his company). You are to find out what schools the man graduated from, what jobs he has held, and whatever you can about his family.

1. Check public records in your city or county for recorded events such as marriage, birth of children, and purchase of a house.

2. See if the schools where the person lived growing up have online lists of alumni (people who graduated from that school) listed by year.

3. Be sure you identify the right person so your information is accurate. There may be several John Smiths on record; you need the John J. Smith who was born in Biloxi and graduated from Duke University in 1987.

4. Check the records of professional associations to help you track the person's work history. For example, doctors, lawyers, engineers, and others belong to associations in different areas of the country. You may be able to track down their employers through these associations.

5. Verify information by checking it with more than one source.

> **"**As a general rule the most successful man in life is the man who has the best information.**"**
> —Benjamin Disraeli, English statesman

# Performance Review

**W**hat rating would an employer give you on acquiring and evaluating information?

- Needs Improvement
- Average

- Above Average
- Outstanding

Take action to earn an Outstanding rating by consistently doing the tasks in the following checklist.

## ACQUIRING AND EVALUATING INFORMATION CHECKLIST

- ◯ Ask questions to determine what information is needed.
- ◯ Use the best research techniques. Know how to find information with Internet search engines, libraries, and other resources.
- ◯ Double-check information by verifying it with a variety of sources. Make sure the sources you use are reliable and current.

# Words at Work

**T**hese words relate to acquiring and evaluating information. How many can you define?

- Acquire
- Evaluate
- Relevance
- Accuracy

- Data
- Sources
- Verify
- Double-check

# ORGANIZING AND MAINTAINING INFORMATION

If you gather a lot of information but have no way to organize or update it on a regular basis, you may have wasted your time. Organizing and maintaining information is a way to make sense of it and keep its value over time.

You can organize information in several ways. You can create tables of data or collect printed information in paper folders and file them alphabetically. Maintaining the organizational system you choose involves keeping the information current and in its proper place.

Organizing and maintaining information includes the ability to

- Organize information in a systematic way
- Process information efficiently
- Maintain written or computerized records

## Careers That Use This Skill

Any worker will do better by having this skill, but these careers are often required to organize and maintain information:

- Librarians
- Database administrators
- Archivists
- Web site designers
- Administrative assistants
- Data entry workers
- Pharmacists
- Court reporters
- Editors
- Writers

# Why Employers Want This Skill

Information is at the core of most businesses today. No matter what career interests you, you are likely to need to organize and maintain information in order to succeed. An important part of this skill is knowing how to use a computer because that is how most employers manage their information.

Many entry-level jobs, such as clerks and administrative assistants, have job duties relating to organizing and maintaining information. These duties include filing, entering data in a computer, sending e-mail, faxing, and making copies. These tasks are necessary to ensure that everyone has access to the information they need to do their jobs, but these tasks also are time-consuming. Employees who can complete these tasks quickly and accurately or who can come up with better ways of organizing and maintaining information will impress their employers. Employees who don't follow their employer's procedures for handling information can cause problems for other workers who need to find that information later.

Organized employees don't waste time looking for important phone numbers or the latest sales figures. They can easily get to the information they need because they establish logical systems for storing the information and regularly update the information. This attention to detail makes it easy for these employees to provide other workers with the information they need as well.

> **❝**It is a capital mistake to theorize before one has data.**❞**
>
> —Sir Arthur Conan Doyle, author

# Organizing and Maintaining Information on the Job

Name: Andy Martinez

Job: Manager of the service plan program for an appliance manufacturer

*Arvid Appliances provides a one-year warranty on all its appliances. It also offers an extended service plan for a fee. When somebody buys an Arvid appliance, he or she sends in a warranty card. Some people purchase the service plan as well. My department has to enter all service plan and warranty information in the system so that if the customer calls about a problem, the customer service department can look up the record. I have three full-time employees who enter this information and maintain the records.*

*Also, just before a warranty expires, my department sends a notice and offers the extended service plan to customers. Of course, my department uses a computerized database of information, which provides a daily report of people whose warranties are about to expire. But somebody has to run the report and make sure the service plan offers are sent.*

*I need people with a good sense of organization to work with all these systems. My three employees are all great at working with procedures to keep information organized, accurate, and up-to-date. I couldn't do without them!*

## Build Your Skills

Look for opportunities in your education and activities to develop your ability to organize and maintain information.

### Education

- Take courses in computers to learn how to use database and spreadsheet software.
- Take a workshop in time and contact management to learn about systems that help you keep track of schedules and people.
- Take a course in office administrative skills to learn about systems of filing and so on.

### Activities

- Volunteer to help in the office of a nonprofit group. You can pick up organizing skills from the full-time staff.
- Keeping up with schoolwork and activities takes a lot of organization. How do you keep track of it all? If you rely on your parents and teachers for reminders, it's time you took charge of your own information. Come up with a system to organize information about your assignments, friends, practices, and other events that works for you and use it!
- Paperwork from school can quickly get out of control. Take a look in your locker, your backpack, and your desk at home. Is there stuff in there you no longer need? Toss it! If you make this a weekly habit, you'll be amazed at how much easier it is to find your homework.

# Try It Yourself

You are working part-time in the office of a local theater company. Your boss presents you with a large box filled with slips of paper and tells you that these are the membership forms from the last three years. She's always wanted somebody to organize them and create a mailing list from them. How would you tackle this job? Here are some tips:

1. Alphabetize the slips. Create dividers for each letter of the alphabet from cardboard or purchase dividers in an office supply store.

2. Consider whether the forms from three years ago are too old to keep in an active file.

3. Enter the names and addresses in a computerized database. Once entered, you can sort the records by the year they were acquired, the zip code, donation amount, and so on.

4. Decide how you will update and add to the information. If you do a mailing, plan to update the list to get rid of addresses for people whose mail comes back as undeliverable, for example. When new members sign up this year, add them to the database promptly.

> **❝**In your thirst for knowledge be sure not to drown in all the information.**❞**
> —Anthony J. D'Angelo, author

# Performance Review

What rating would an employer give you on organizing and maintaining information?

- Needs Improvement
- Average
- Above Average
- Outstanding

Take action to earn an Outstanding rating by consistently doing the tasks in the following checklist.

---

## ORGANIZING AND MAINTAINING INFORMATION CHECKLIST

○ Choose a system of organizing your information that makes it easy to find the information you need.

○ Use procedures and reminders to help you update information.

○ Always handle information according to the systems and procedures that are in place.

---

# Words at Work

These words relate to organizing and maintaining information. How many can you define?

- Clerical
- Process
- Maintain
- Classify
- Records
- Procedure
- Database
- Systematic

# INTERPRETING AND COMMUNICATING INFORMATION

Every day, information comes at you from all directions. But until you interpret what that information means, it is not that useful.

Once you analyze and interpret information, you may need to communicate that interpretation to others. You can communicate information to people in a variety of ways. For example, you might give a speech, send out an e-mail, or prepare a presentation that involves video and animation.

Interpreting and communicating information includes the ability to

- Select appropriate information
- Analyze the information
- Communicate your analysis of information to others
- Use various methods of communication including speech, writing, graphics, and multimedia

## Careers That Use This Skill

Any worker will do better by having this skill, but these careers are often required to interpret and communicate information:

- Market researchers
- Journalists
- Financial analysts
- Medical diagnosticians
- Analysts
- Dispatchers
- Doctors
- Teachers
- Marketing managers

# Why Employers Want This Skill

Information is at the heart of most organizations today. How well you make sense of it and communicate it can make a big difference in how well you do your job. Doctors, for example, must be able to figure out what disease a patient has from doing a physical examination and looking at test results. They then must be able to explain this information to the patient in terms that he or she can understand. Lawyers have to be able to present evidence and argue their cases in such a way that the jury understands their message. Charity organizations have to collect information about the people they help and the people who still need help. They then have to communicate that information in written proposals or television commercials, for example, to encourage foundations and individuals to donate money.

No matter what job you have, you will have to interpret and communicate information for your boss, your coworkers, and your customers. This skill is especially important in jobs that are highly specialized and technical because they involve information that other people may find difficult to understand. If you communicate information that is important to your audience in a way that they find useful, they will be impressed with your abilities.

> **"There are no facts, only interpretations."**
> —Frederich Nietzche, philosopher

# Interpreting and Communicating Information on the Job

Name: Sandra Martinez

Job: Marketing director for a shipbuilding company

*Chandler Shipbuilding is a mid-sized shipbuilding company located in the Northeast. Each year it holds an annual meeting for stockholders. At that meeting the company's managers have to present information about the company's products, profits, and so on.*

*The members of my staff have to assemble information about sales, revenues, and so on from the accounting department. Then, they create an annual report that presents the information in words, charts, and tables. They also create a multimedia presentation that highlights the company's successes. Together these materials communicate a message about the past year that helps the stockholders understand the company's current situation.*

*I count on people in accounting to compile the information and the people in my department to interpret it and communicate it in the annual report and presentation. We pull the facts together and present them in an exciting and easy-to-understand way.*

# Build Your Skills

Look for opportunities in your education and activities to develop your ability to interpret and communicate information.

### Education

- Take courses in speech and communication to learn about communicating with others.

- Take a class in videography or graphic design to learn how to present information effectively using multimedia and graphics.

- Study statistics to discover how to analyze numbers and other data so you can spot trends.

### Activities

- Participate in a science fair. Science fairs require you to interpret the information you gather from the experiments you perform. You then have to create a display that presents the details of your experiment in a clear and appealing way. You may also have to verbally present your data and conclusions to several judges.

- Raise awareness about an issue that's important to you, such as animal cruelty, drunk driving, or homelessness. You could draw a poster, create a skit, or write a radio announcement. Before you start, consider who your audience will be. Will it be students at your school, parents and teachers, or kindergarteners? How does your audience affect the information you include and how you communicate it?

# Try It Yourself

**Y**ou work in the marketing department of a magazine publisher. The publisher wants to announce a new line of online magazines, which are called e-zines. Your boss has asked you to gather information about other e-zines' marketing and make suggestions about the best way to promote your new products.

How would you approach this job? Here are some tips:

1.  Research what others have done. You can search online, visit other publisher's Web sites, and study other e-zines. Try to find out which marketing strategies were most successful.

2.  Take a look at the best ways to reach your potential audience. Do they spend a lot of time online, or are most of your potential subscribers already subscribers to your print magazines?

3.  Find a way to organize your data so it is easy to analyze. Use tables, charts, or whatever other methods you can find to put information in a logical context.

4.  Create a presentation for your boss providing the information you collected on competitors and your audience. Decide whether you should you use charts, animated presentations, a printed document, or some other media to communicate what you've learned.

> **"**One has only to spend an hour looking at papers written by graduate students to realize the extent to which the ability to communicate is not universally held.**"**
> —Gerald Weinberg, author

## Performance Review

**W**hat rating would an employer give you on interpreting and communicating information?

- Needs Improvement
- Average

- Above Average
- Outstanding

Take action to earn an Outstanding rating by consistently doing the tasks in the following checklist.

---

### INTERPRETING AND COMMUNICATING INFORMATION CHECKLIST

◯ Decide which information is most important for your purpose.

◯ Clearly connect your conclusions and analysis to the facts.

◯ Present information in a format that appeals to your audience.

---

## Words at Work

**T**hese words relate to interpreting and communicating information. How many can you define?

- Interpret
- Analyze
- Graphic
- Multimedia

- Convey
- Disseminate
- Media
- Relevant

# USING COMPUTERS TO PROCESS INFORMATION

No matter what your job, you are likely to use computers. You may research information on the Internet. Perhaps you will use a program to do calculations or write business letters. You will probably have to use e-mail at some point to communicate with coworkers. Because you are likely to use computers to process information in a job someday, it's important that you start learning this skill right away. Using a computer to process information includes the ability to

- Find information with computers
- Organize information with a computer program
- Analyze information using a computer
- Communicate information using a computer

## Careers That Use This Skill

Any worker will do better by having this skill, but people in these careers are often required to use computers to process information:

- Database administrators
- Webmasters
- Accountants
  - Paralegals
    - Medical researchers
- Scientists
- Tax preparers
- Desktop publishers
- Computer software engineers

# Why Employers Want This Skill

Twenty-five years ago, few workers used computers. Only in the 1980s did desktop computers come into common use. Since then, they have become essential to doing business around the world. Computers are used to design plans for buildings and streets in cities, store millions of customer addresses, and keep track of inventory.

Computer training is expensive, so most employers want to hire employees who already have computer knowledge and don't require additional training. In most office environments, employees are expected to have at least a basic knowledge of word processing, spread-sheet, presentation, and e-mail software. In addition, workers need to know the most common software used in their career field. For exam-ple, a graphic designer needs to know how to use photo editing and page layout software.

Computer software is updated often, so you will need to stay on top of changes in software that relates to your career in order to be success-ful. Your employer may send you to training to upgrade your skills, or you may have to take classes on your own to stay competitive. If you become an expert user of computer software, not only will you be able to enter, retrieve, and organize information quickly, but you will also become a more valuable worker because you can help other workers use the software.

> **"** I do not fear computers. I fear the lack of them. **"**
> —E. W. Dijkstra, computer pioneer

# Using Computers to Process Information on the Job

Name: Art Pendragon

Job: Owner of a taxi service

*My company, Wellington Taxi Service, has a fleet of taxis that operates all around this city. The dispatchers use a computer to locate hard-to-find addresses and give the drivers directions. Next year I'm going to invest in an onboard system that drivers can use to find addresses themselves. That means just about everybody who works for me will have to be comfortable using a simple computer system to get information.*

*One of my dispatchers, Mark Wong, really enjoys working with computers. He came up with a Web site that provides detailed directions from one address in the city to another. It's been a big help. That Web site accounts for things like one-way streets and street closures that aren't marked on printed maps.*

*Another cool way our drivers use computers is to process credit cards. They have a little terminal in the taxi and can run the charge right there using a wireless connection to the computer in the office. Because the charge comes through the office, I can tally all of a driver's credit card sales at the end of the day before the driver even returns to the garage.*

*You might not have thought taxi drivers would use a computer to do their work, but they do. I always ask people applying for a job now if they are comfortable using computers.*

# Build Your Skills

Look for opportunities in your education and activities to develop your ability to use computers to process information.

## Education

- Take courses in computers to learn about their various features.
- Take a class in using a particular software to expand your computer skills. If you learn to program, you can even create your own software!
- Take an online course to see what advances are being made in teaching people over the Internet.

## Activities

- The next time you use a computer, check to see how many programs you know how to use. Can you use a music player, a Web browser, a calculator, a word processor, and a game? You may know more programs than you realize.
- With the career that interests you in mind, search the Internet to see what kinds of software programs a person in that job might use. Learn a couple of those programs this year.
- Practice using the computer to communicate. Next time you send an e-mail message, for example, try adding attachments such as pictures or documents. You can also use instant messaging to talk to a friend online.

# Try It Yourself

You work in the fund-raising department of a large arts center. Your boss asks you to use a new database program to organize the contributors' records. How would you approach this task? You could

1. Use the computer to update contributors' addresses from Internet phone directories.

2. Input contributor records into a database program and use sorting and filtering features to organize the information.

3. Run reports to analyze the information. For example, how many of your contributors live in the city, and how many in the suburbs?

4. Print out or e-mail reports to your boss to share the information you have gathered and analyzed.

> **"**Computer science is no more about computers than astronomy is about telescopes.**"**
> —Isaac Asimov, author

## Performance Review

What rating would an employer give you on using computers to process information?

- Needs Improvement
- Average
- Above Average
- Outstanding

Take action to earn an Outstanding rating by consistently doing the tasks in the following checklist.

> ### USING COMPUTERS TO PROCESS INFORMATION CHECKLIST
>
> ◯ Use a variety of search techniques to quickly find information with a computer.
>
> ◯ Know how to use the tools of common computer programs to organize and analyze information.
>
> ◯ Be professional when using computers to communicate information.

## Words at Work

These words relate to using computers to process information. How many can you define?

- Analyze
- Program
- Software
- Database
- Spreadsheet
- Browser
- E-mail
- Filter

# UNDERSTANDING SYSTEMS

A system is a set of procedures used to accomplish something. Think of the systems in your school. The school library uses the Dewey decimal system to organize the books. Your teachers use a system to discipline students who misbehave; perhaps such students are sent to another class for think time or to the principal's office.

Understanding and working within systems is a valuable skill to develop for your future career. Understanding systems includes the ability to

- Recognize how social and organizational systems work
- Understand procedural and technology systems
- Work effectively within systems

## Careers That Use This Skill

Any worker will do better by having this skill, but people in these careers are often required to understand and work within systems:

- Librarians
- Information technology workers
- Bookkeepers
- Cost estimators
- Air traffic controllers
- Lab technicians
- Architects

# Why Employers Want This Skill

Systems are used in the workplace in all kinds of ways. There are systems for hiring and firing people, systems for training people, systems for filing paperwork, systems for computer security, and so on. Systems help people know how to behave and what to expect of each other on the job. Being able to work within systems is an important part of many jobs.

Employees work to help their employers achieve their goals. In order to do the best job, employees must understand what their employers' goals are and how their jobs function in the organization. For example, the goal of a fast-food restaurant is to make money by meeting their customer's expectations for food quality and fast service. Cooks at these restaurants have to follow certain procedures to make the food. If they don't, the food will take longer to cook and won't taste the way the customer expects it to, and the unhappy customer will stop buying food at that restaurant.

Employees who understand how their actions affect other parts of the organization are usually more motivated to do a good job and are more likely to come up with ideas about how systems can be improved. Managers, in particular, need a good understanding of systems to help their departments run smoothly and perform well with the other parts of the organization.

> **"**It is best to do things systematically, since we are only human, and disorder is our worst enemy.**"**
> —Hesiod, ancient Greek poet

# Understanding Systems on the Job

Name: Lindy Myanmar

Job: Manufacturing supervisor for a toy company

*When I hire a new person to work on the Paisley Toy Company manufacturing line, I ask questions to help me understand how well this person works with systems because Paisley Toy has a lot of them. For example, there's a system for assembling parts and a system for reporting safety incidents. There's even a system for requesting a change to the system!*

*Don't get me wrong: I like systems. Systems let everybody know what to expect. When all of us on the line do certain things the same way, things stay consistent. That's how we get the job done. It's important that we also find ways for people to do some things their own way, but following systems is what this operation is based on.*

*People who can't get the hang of systems have trouble getting up to speed. They don't understand the logic underlying the system. They can't understand the structure of the company. Eventually they get up to speed, but the people who catch on right away are especially valuable to the company, especially when a new system comes in.*

> **"**First comes thought; then organization of that thought, into ideas and plans; then transformation of those plans into reality.**"**
>
> —Napoleon Hill, author

# Build Your Skills

**U**nderstanding systems can involve several abilities, including organization, planning, and following directions. Look for opportunities in your education and activities to develop these abilities.

## Education

- Take science classes to study systems in nature, such as the ecosystem or solar system.

- In social studies classes, note the different social and organizational systems that groups use. Compare the economic, governmental, and educational systems used in different countries and during different times in history. What are the results of those systems?

## Activities

- Look at the procedures you follow in an activity you're involved in. Figure out how you could improve these procedures and suggest these changes to others who are involved.

- Study systems in the world today. How do we pay taxes, apply for college, or get a loan? What are the steps in those systems and why and how do you think they were developed? Imagine what would happen if there were no system in place.

- Get a few sets of instructions for procedures and compare them. You might find an employee handbook for a business, or a guide to installing a home entertainment center, or a book on designing a birdhouse. Which procedures are better than others? Why?

# Try It Yourself

**U**nderstanding systems means understanding the logic underlying the systems. You have to see why following the system keeps the procedure well-organized and efficient. (Of course, some systems are more logical than others; if you have to use one that isn't logical, suggest improvements!)

Suppose you have started work as a lab technician at a large hospital. Although you have had training, this is your first job in a hospital setting. There are several very important procedures for handling medical specimens that you have to learn. How would you approach this job? Here are some tips:

1. Study any written guidelines for procedures that are available.

2. The first time you work with a system, ask somebody to show it to you. Then try it yourself with an experienced person looking on.

3. Make a list of the steps in the system and identify the purpose of each one. Even if there is good written documentation, your notes will put things into your own words and help you remember them.

4. Look at the system in light of the larger goals of your organization. The more you can understand the underlying logic of the system, the easier it is to remember to follow it. Figure out the need for the system and the goal of those who created it. Ask people why the system exists and listen carefully to their answers. Try to understand who uses the system and what each person gets out of using it.

5. Identify the results of using the system and recognize the value of these results to the organization.

# Performance Review

What rating would an employer give you on understanding systems?

- Needs Improvement
- Average
- Above Average
- Outstanding

Take action to earn an Outstanding rating by consistently doing the tasks in the following checklist.

## UNDERSTANDING SYSTEMS CHECKLIST

- ◯ Learn the reasons for the systems you work with.
- ◯ Use both written and verbal assistance in learning a system and take notes as you learn.
- ◯ Repeat the steps of the system often to make them second nature.

# Words at Work

These words relate to understanding systems. How many can you define?

- Routine
- Regulation
- Structure
- Categorize
- Method
- Pattern
- Consistent
- Logic

# MONITORING AND CORRECTING PERFORMANCE

**W**hy do people go to the doctor for yearly physicals or take their cars in for regular tune-ups? They want to make sure that the systems they rely on are working the way they should. At some point, most systems do not function in the way they are expected to. The only way to catch these problems is to regularly check the system. Once you pinpoint the problem, you then have to take steps to correct it.

Monitoring and correcting system performance involves the following:

- Identifying trends in system performance
- Predicting the impact of actions on systems
- Recognizing changes in the function of a system
- Making adjustments to correct performance

## Careers That Use This Skill

**A**ny worker will do better by having this skill, but these careers are often required to monitor and correct performance:

- Inspectors
- Construction managers
- Teachers
- Engineers
- Efficiency experts
- Financial planners
- Editors
- Industrial production managers

## Why Employers Want This Skill

**O**ften, an organization's greatest strengths are its systems. For example, the government and economic systems of the United States have helped it to become a strong and wealthy country. When a system breaks down, the result can be disastrous. If workers fail to follow safety procedures, for example, they could injure themselves or others.

Employers cannot just set up systems and then walk away. The more important the system is, the more closely it needs to be monitored. To monitor system problems, supervisors often compare results to benchmarks. Benchmarks are the results a system produces when everything is working perfectly. Suppose you own a candy factory that can ideally produce 10,000 chocolate bars a day, but it has only been producing about 7,000 bars a day for the past couple of weeks. Fewer chocolate bars means fewer sales. If you didn't monitor the chocolate production system, you could be losing money without even knowing it!

Finding the problem is one thing; fixing it is another. Employees who see the potential for problems and know what to do to prevent those problems from occurring are very valuable to their employers. These employees help their employers avoid minor mishaps and major losses every day.

> **❝**A man who has committed a mistake and doesn't correct it is committing another mistake. **❞**
> —Confucius, philosopher

# Monitoring and Correcting Performance on the Job

Name: Melody Constantine

Job: Human resources manager

*I run the human resources department here at Polyphony, a sheet music publisher. I put a system in place a few years ago for performance reviews. Each manager had to fill out a form and give an in-person review to every employee twice a year. The employee's salary increases and bonuses were tied to the review.*

*When Polyphony bought another company, MusicTone Publishers, I put the Polyphony review system in place for the employees from MusicTone so that everyone would be using the same review system. However, a lot of managers from MusicTone had trouble meeting the performance review deadlines.*

*I asked one of my employees, Sandy, to analyze the problem. He asked the MusicTone managers questions about the review system they had used in the past and how it worked. He discovered that the problem was paperwork. MusicTone had a computerized system for reviews. Filling out forms manually and mailing them into the Polyphony headquarters in another city took more time than they were used to and caused them to miss deadlines. Sandy recommended that we change everybody to MusicTone's computerized system because it was faster, and I agreed. Now my department is able to record salary changes much faster, which makes the employees happy.*

# Build Your Skills

Look for opportunities in your education and activities to develop your skill in monitoring and correcting system performance.

**Education**

- Study situations in history where a system stopped performing as expected. For example, has there been a natural disaster in the world recently where the emergency response system did not work effectively? How could those in charge identify and correct the problem?

- Take science classes. The study of science involves using a system known as the scientific method to gain knowledge about the world. By doing experiments, you can practice observing and analyzing natural systems.

**Activities**

- Study a system in your school. Ask questions about when and why it was started. Can you see any flaws in the system? Watch how it performs over several weeks. When does it work best? Why? Does the system work better when some people are using it and not so well when others use it?

- Your body is full of systems, such as the digestive system, the nervous system, and the respiratory system. Pick a system and find out as much as you can about it by reading books and searching on the Internet. What can you do to make sure those systems are working the way they should? Can you make them work better?

- Take note of the systems your family has in place for accomplishing tasks. Who is in charge of monitoring these systems? Are there times when these systems don't work they way they should? What happens when the systems fail?

# Try It Yourself

You are a computer network administrator in a large manufacturing company. You generate reports every week on the network's performance. Recently you've noticed that the system is performing more slowly than usual. How would you deal with this situation? Here are some tips:

1. Do more research to figure out whether users are doing different things with the system. For example, has the company added employees and computers to the system or has a new software program been installed?

2. Analyze the data you collect. If you see that the system performs fine at night when employees are not using it much, but it freezes up first thing in the morning when everybody logs into the computers, this might help you pinpoint the problem.

3. Suggest solutions to your boss and take corrective action. You may request a change to the work system so users don't access demanding operations all at the same time, for example. Or you may suggest that your network software be upgraded to a newer version.

4. Keep an eye on the system when the changes are in place. Has the change fixed the problem?

> **"** Mistakes, obviously, show us what needs improving. Without mistakes, how would we know what we had to work on? **"**
>
> —Peter McWilliams, author

# Performance Review

**W**hat rating would an employer give you on monitoring and correcting performance?

- Needs Improvement
- Average
- Above Average
- Outstanding

Take action to earn an Outstanding rating by consistently doing the tasks in the following checklist.

---

## MONITORING AND CORRECTING PERFORMANCE CHECKLIST

○ Communicate with people who use the system. If they understand how the system is intended to work, they can help spot problems when they occur.

○ Set a range of acceptable system results. Take action when the results fall below the minimum that is acceptable.

---

# Words at Work

**T**hese words relate to monitoring and correcting system performance. How many can you define?

- Monitor
- Benchmark
- Assess
- Distinguish
- Diagnose
- Standards
- Remedy
- Deviate

# IMPROVING AND DESIGNING SYSTEMS

**S**ystem procedures aren't perfect. They may need to be improved, possibly because changes in the workplace have made them less efficient than they once were. Sometimes an entirely new system is needed. Perhaps a task that was once simple and done by one person has become more complex and involves more people. Now the company needs a system so that everybody knows how to perform the task in the same way.

Improving existing systems and designing new systems can be interesting and rewarding. These skills involve the ability to

- Make suggestions to modify existing systems
- Find ways to improve products or services
- Develop new or alternative systems

## Careers That Use This Skill

**A**ny worker will do better by having this skill, but these careers are often required to improve or design systems:

- Engineers
- Architects
- Industrial production managers
- Scientists
- Urban planners
- Electricians

# Why Employers Want This Skill

The economy and the world are always changing, so organizations must constantly review what they are doing and how they are doing it in order to stay competitive and successful. People who can contribute improvements to systems offer a valuable skill to employers.

Many issues are involved in changing or creating a system. System designers must first look at the logical order for doing things in the system. Some things must be done before others can be done; some things can be done at the same time, but only if enough people are available to do them simultaneously. In addition, there may be costs associated with the steps in the system. System designers must look for ways to keep those costs down. Employees who are not comfortable with designing or improving systems may hang on to outdated systems for too long and cost their employers time and money.

To design new systems well, you must have a good sense of organization and detail. You also have to be able to create a system that will work within your organization. A good way to earn promotions and raises at work is to come up with ways to improve systems that save your employer time or money. If you see a need for a completely new system, you can impress your employers by developing good procedures for that system.

> **"**Order, unity, and continuity are human inventions just as truly as catalogues and encyclopedias. **"**
> —Bertrand Russell, philosopher

# Improving and Designing Systems on the Job

Name: Ralph Enero

Job: Operations manager

*I manage the plant and offices for Perky Pet Foods. It's my job to make sure things run smoothly around here. If employees want to arrange repairs on a machine or order a new sign or office furniture, they come to me. I also negotiate the office space lease and other things like that.*

*I have a staff of three people to help out. When I hired Marty, he took our requisition system and totally revamped it. First he identified the logical steps in making a request, and then he chose the most efficient way to do it. It used to take about five steps to order a new desk chair or carpet repair; now it takes two. That saves Perky Pet Foods time and money and helps employees avoid mistakes that lots of steps can introduce.*

*Another one of my people, Lacey, worked with the phone company people to set up an entirely new system for answering the telephones. While she was designing the system, she focused on the people who would have to use the system to make sure their needs were met. The new system allows callers to locate a person using an automated directory. That saves our receptionist a lot of time. Thanks to Lacey's smart design and her work with the phone company, the system is also easy to understand and follow.*

*People like Marty and Lacey who can design or improve systems make operations at Perky Pet Foods go more smoothly and often save the company money.*

# Build Your Skills

Improving and designing systems can involve several abilities, including organization, planning, and good communication. You can develop this skill through your education and activities.

### Education

- Take courses in business to learn about examples of successful systems.

- Take science classes to study systems used to perform experiments and develop theories.

- Take a course in time or project management to see how systems help save time or money.

### Activities

- Identify a system you work with at school. How could the system be improved on? Could it be done in fewer steps or be made easier for the people using it?

- Create a new system for a family activity. For example, if everybody fights over who does which chore, create a schedule for distributing chores that everybody can follow.

- Interview the adults you know about systems they use at work. Do they find some of the systems frustrating? Are the systems difficult to learn? Ask them whether they have suggested improvements to systems. Have they ever had to design a system from scratch?

- Tour a factory to observe systems in action. Ask your guide how the product was made when the company first started. Has technology changed the way the factory operates now?

# Try It Yourself

You have been asked to create a system for using an online calendar program at your company to schedule meetings. The program offers several options for how it can be used and you have to figure out the best setup for your company. How would you approach this job? Here are some tips:

1. Study any currently successful systems used in the company to see what makes them work well.

2. Make a list of everybody who will need to use the automated calendar system and make sure everybody has access to it on his or her computer.

3. Ask people how they schedule meetings now; there may be elements of the current manual system that could be included in the automated system.

4. Consider what it will take to teach people to use the new system. A system that nobody understands is of little use!

> **❝**You know you've achieved perfection in design, not when you have nothing more to add, but when you have nothing more to take away.**❞**
> —Antoine de Saint-Exupery, author

# Performance Review

What rating would an employer give you on improving and designing systems?

- Needs Improvement
- Average
- Above Average
- Outstanding

Take action to earn an Outstanding rating by consistently doing the tasks in the following checklist.

## IMPROVING AND DESIGNING SYSTEMS CHECKLIST

- ○ Identify each step of the system to find places for improvement.
- ○ Consider the way people like to work.
- ○ Make plans to put the system in place, including training people to use it.

# Words at Work

These words relate to improving and designing systems. How many can you define?

- Revamp
- Effective
- Process
- Overhaul
- Order
- Interact
- Efficient
- Timing

# SELECTING TECHNOLOGY

Technology is the process of using specialized knowledge or tools to accomplish a task. The world today is filled with technology to help you do just about anything. However, the amount of available technology can sometimes be overwhelming, which is why selecting the right technology has become an important career skill. Selecting technology involves understanding what you want the technology to do and finding what technology is available that can do what you want.

Selecting technology includes the ability to

- Judge which set of procedures, tools, or machines will produce the desired results
- Select computers and programs that meet an organization's needs
- Project technology needs of the future

## Careers That Use This Skill

Any worker will do better by having this skill, but people in these careers are often required to select technology:

- Network administrators
- Managers
- Health technologists
- Business consultants
- Engineers
- Scientists
- Education administrators

# Why Employers Want This Skill

Perhaps you think that technology is something that only computer programmers or scientists deal with, but technology is everywhere in the workplace. The future will bring technology into even more hands and more job descriptions. For example, if you are a receptionist, you might be asked to research and recommend a software program to schedule meetings. If you run an auto repair shop, you use a computer to diagnose the problem with a car, and you have to purchase that computer system. If you manage a grocery store, you have to choose a scanning system to automatically update the inventory in the store.

Cost is a major issue to consider when selecting technology. Not everybody can afford the best technology, but no employer wants to buy something that is so low cost and low quality that it's practically useless. Employers also don't want to waste thousands of dollars on technology that has lots of features they don't need or that is going to become out-of-date in one or two years. For these reasons, employers need employees who can make smart buying decisions concerning technology.

Reliability and usability are important issues, too. Technology often has to be maintained, updated, and repaired. You should make sure the technology you select will not pose problems in these areas. In addition, if the technology is difficult to use, it won't save you or your coworkers any time. It might even just create more work when you spend hours trying to figure out how to use it. Employers need employees who can select technology that works for the people who will be using it.

# Selecting Technology on the Job

Name: Julie Metzger

Job: Office manager

*The operation of the office for Janson Advertising is in my hands. That includes choosing furnishings, planning the phone system, and purchasing service contracts for equipment such as copiers.*

*Last year, the company decided to put in a new phone system. The company was growing so fast that the employees needed features such as an automated directory, caller ID, conferencing, and so on. I was the one responsible for choosing the system. The first thing I did was sit down and make a list of the features the company needed. I asked the other employees what features they would like to have to make sure that I didn't forget anything.*

*Then I talked to several companies who deal in phone systems. I had to weigh technical features against other factors such as cost, quality, and support. Some companies had one feature but not the others. A few had everything Janson Advertising needed, but they didn't offer very good technical support or the cost was too high. One company had the perfect combination that would meet Janson's needs. The quality of their phone equipment was great, and the process required to program and reprogram the system was something that Janson employees could do themselves.*

*I learned a lot about telephone technology in the process of choosing a new phone system. Making the decision was a matter of first identifying what Janson needed technology to do and then finding a match instead of making my coworkers live with technology that couldn't do what the business needed.*

# Build Your Skills

Selecting technology can involve several abilities, including budgeting, analyzing, and understanding the technology. You can develop these abilities through your education and activities.

**Education**

- Take courses in computers to learn about computer equipment and software.
- Take courses in electronics to learn how machines work.

**Activities**

- Join a club that involves an electrical or mechanical hobby such as fixing up old cars or building robots. When you understand how one machine works, you can often generalize that information to other machines.
- Pick a technology such as computers, wireless phones, or GPS and learn everything you can about it. Use the Internet, buy books, or just ask people what they know.
- Shop for an electronic gift for someone. Consider what the person would use the most and how comfortable the person is with technology. For example, your music-loving grandmother might not be ready for an MP3 player, but she might like a CD changer for her stereo system. You also need to consider how much money you have to spend.

> **"**Humanity is acquiring all the right technology for all the wrong reasons. **"**
>
> —R. Buckminster Fuller, inventor and futurist

# Try It Yourself

You work in a mid-sized law firm and have been asked to choose a new copier for your office. How would you approach this job? Here are some tips:

1. Talk to people in your office to find out how they will use the copier and what they like and don't like about the existing copy machine.

2. Gather some information about available copiers and make a list of the features that they have that you think are needed at your company. Use the Internet, or ask vendors to provide brochures.

3. Consider other issues such as how you will train people to use the new machine, what kind of support or service contract is offered, and the repair record of the equipment.

4. Ask questions about and research the latest developments in the technology. Are there new features coming soon and should you wait for them? If you tried to replace a VCR today, for example, you would want to know that fewer and fewer movie distributors are releasing movies in that format today. If the most current technology is DVDs, why buy a new VCR?

> **"**The first rule of any technology used in a business is that automation applied to an efficient operation will magnify the efficiency. The second is that automation applied to an inefficient operation will magnify the inefficiency.**"**
>
> —Bill Gates, founder of Microsoft Corporation

# Performance Review

**W**hat rating would an employer give you on selecting technology?

- Needs Improvement
- Average
- Above Average
- Outstanding

Take action to earn an Outstanding rating by consistently doing the tasks in the following checklist.

---

## SELECTING TECHNOLOGY CHECKLIST

○ Gather information about the technology from companies making or selling the technology and from people writing about the technology.

○ Evaluate whether the technology fits your organization in terms of cost, reliability, and features.

○ Make plans to put the technology in place, including training people to use it.

---

# Words at Work

**T**hese words relate to selecting technology. How many can you define?

- Software
- Hardware
- Automate
- Network
- Technology
- Machinery
- Cutting-edge
- Obsolete

# APPLYING TECHNOLOGY

From the time you wake up in the morning until you go to bed at night, you use technology to get things done. You set an alarm clock to wake you up at the right time, use a microwave to make snacks, and push buttons on a remote control to find something good to watch on television. As you go through life, you will continue to learn how to use machines to accomplish things at home and at work. An important part of preparing for a career is learning how to apply the technology you will use on the job.

Applying technology includes the ability to

- Set up machines
- Operate machines
- Use computers

## Careers That Use This Skill

Any worker will do better by having this skill, but people in these careers are often required to apply technology:

- Computer programmers
- Scientists
- Machinists
    - Engineers
    - Production occupations
- Construction equipment operators
- Medical imaging technicians
- Repairers

# Why Employers Want This Skill

**K**nowing when and how to apply a particular technology to a task is important in many jobs. For example, if you are an office worker, you have to choose which software to use to create a document. If you are a carpenter, you have to know which tool is best for a particular job. If you run a machine shop, you have to set up and operate machinery.

Employers want employees who are comfortable with technology and who can easily adapt to new technology. In some cases, the manufacturer of the new technology will set it up for you. (For example, if your parents buy a washing machine, the people who deliver it will often set it up.) In other cases, you have to read a manual to learn how to set it up yourself.

To some extent you will learn about a particular technology when you need it on the job. Sometimes you will have a manual or other information to help you, and sometimes somebody at your company will teach you to use a piece of equipment or computer. But getting familiar with technologies in the area of your career interest now will help you apply that technology down the road.

> **"**The number one benefit of information technology is that it empowers people to do what they want to do. It lets people be creative. It lets people be productive. It lets people learn things they didn't think they could learn before, and so in a sense it is all about potential. **"**
> —Steve Ballmer, CEO of Microsoft Corporation

# Applying Technology on the Job

Name: Randy Leavenworth

Job: Vice president of sales

*I run the sales operation here at Delica Chocolates, Inc., and I manage 10 salespeople. Each salesperson is assigned to a set of accounts including large department stores, grocery store chains, and so on. In the past when somebody took an order, that information was faxed to the office. Then somebody else had to input it into the computer system. Sometimes the fax wouldn't come through. Sometimes people typing in the order made mistakes. The system had problems.*

*Last year my sales manager, Ricky Henshaw had an idea. Ricky suggested that the company buy this new style of computer for the salespeople. This thing is about the size of a legal pad. They can write their orders on the screen itself using a special pen. Then they can send the order into the office instantly using a wireless connection. They get a confirmation that it's been received in an e-mail so no orders get lost. Then the order goes directly into the system, so nobody has to retype it.*

*I'll tell you, the money, time, and mistakes that the new system saved the company is amazing. I gave Ricky a promotion and a raise when I started to see how well the technology worked for the salespeople. People who can see how technology might help in their jobs and know how to put it in place are great to have on my team.*

# Build Your Skills

**L**ook for opportunities to develop your ability to apply technology.

## Education

- Take courses in computers to learn about how to set up and use computer software.

- Take courses in shop, electronics, or automotive technology to learn how machines work.

## Activities

- Learn to use a new piece of technology that you have access to. For example, ask your parents to show you how to use their cell phone or handheld computing device. Read the manual to learn about the various features and potential problems you might encounter.

- If you are comfortable using computers, volunteer to help someone who is uncomfortable using computers. For example, you could show an older relative how to use e-mail to stay in touch with the family. You also could offer to install educational software on a computer for kindergarteners.

- Try a hobby that uses machinery in some way. For example, you can make yourself some shorts on a sewing machine or create your own movies on a digital video recorder. Use kitchen appliances to prepare dinner for your family or a drill to make some shelves for your room. Before you touch any of these machines, however, have an adult show you how to operate them and explain the safety rules you need to follow to protect yourself.

## Try It Yourself

**Y**ou run a small home business and have bought a new fax machine. You have to set it up and get it working. How would you approach this task? Here are some tips:

1. Look at any documentation that comes with the fax machine. There may be a quick-start guide to help you understand how to set it up. The documentation may also include safety warnings.

2. If you have problems getting the machine to work, look for any troubleshooting tips in the documentation, or go to the manufacturer's Web site for advice.

3. When you operate the machine, be sure you use all the features correctly. It may take a while to become comfortable with using it. Be prepared to make modifications to the setup if things don't work exactly as you need them to.

4. If the equipment malfunctions, contact the manufacturer for support. Typically, you can do this through its Web site or through a customer support phone number.

Keep in mind that technology changes and evolves all the time. The technology that will be used in a career 10 years from now will be very different from what's being used today. Staying on top of technology in your field is an ongoing process.

> **"**Advances in technology will continue to reach far into every sector of our economy.**"**
> —Christopher Bond, senator

## Performance Review

**W**hat rating would an employer give you on applying technology?

- Needs Improvement
- Average
- Above Average
- Outstanding

Take action to earn an Outstanding rating by consistently doing the tasks in the following checklist.

---

### APPLYING TECHNOLOGY CHECKLIST

○ Set up the technology to operate the way you need it to.

○ Study any supporting materials to learn how to operate the technology.

○ Know whom to call and what to ask if you have to get repairs, maintenance, or information.

---

## Words at Work

**T**hese words relate to applying technology. How many can you define?

- Program
- Device
- Apparatus
- Application
- Implement
- Utilize
- Operate
- Documentation

# MAINTAINING AND TROUBLESHOOTING TECHNOLOGY

**E**ven the most reliable technology eventually breaks down or wears out, and you may be the only one available to fix the problem. Maintaining technology in part involves trying to prevent problems before they start by checking to make sure everything is working the way it should. When a problem occurs, you can troubleshoot to find out what caused the problem and then fix the part that is broken.

Maintaining and troubleshooting technology includes the ability to

- Prevent problems in machines, computers, and other technologies
- Identify problems with technology
- Solve problems with machines, computers, or other technologies

## Careers That Use This Skill

**A**ny worker will do better by having this skill, but people in these careers are often required to maintain and troubleshoot technology:

- Computer network administrators
- Mechanics
- Service technicians
- Repairers

- Engineers
- Custodians
- Computer support specialists

# Why Employers Want This Skill

Technology is everywhere in the workplace. You will encounter machines such as computers, fax machines, or even robots that assemble parts in a factory. Whether you want to work closely with technology or just use it as a tool to get your job done, learning some basics about maintaining and troubleshooting technology is helpful.

When technology is not working correctly, employees are unable to do their jobs effectively. In larger companies, specific people are assigned to keep technology running. In smaller companies, each employee may be called on to maintain or repair a machine such as a copier or troubleshoot a computer problem.

No matter what you want to do with your life, being comfortable working with technology, especially when it causes problems, is a useful quality to have. If you have good troubleshooting skills, you can prevent minor technology problems from getting in the way of your work. These skills will also make you valuable to coworkers with technology problems. If you have the skills to solve major problems with technology, you will be able to earn a higher salary because there is a high demand for these skills.

> **"**It is only when they go wrong that machines remind you how powerful they are.**"**
> —Clive James, author

# Maintaining and Troubleshooting Technology on the Job

Name: Calyn Brodie

Job: Grocery store manager

*Today's grocery store is full of technology, and Shopper's Mart is no exception. For example, we use these laser devices to scan inventory on shelves. The cash registers are basically computers, and each check-out lane has a terminal for processing credit cards. The office has a computer, copier, and fax machine.*

*But Shopper's Mart is not a big corporation where there's somebody working full time keeping the computers and other machines running. Some machines have a service contract, like the copier. So someone in the office does the basic maintenance, such as adding ink or clearing out paper jams, and calls the service guy in if there's a big problem. But when other machines, such as the computer or fax machine, break down, it's up to me to make sure the problem is fixed. Usually, I try to troubleshoot it because having a professional repairer fix the problem can take a lot of time and money.*

*Fortunately, I also have a couple of employees who are handy with machines. For example, if the inventory scanner stops working right, I see whether Carlos or Tomika is working. One of them can usually figure it out. Having folks like them around in an emergency is very important, especially with a 24-hour operation like Shopper's Mart. Try finding a repairman at 2 a.m.!*

# Build Your Skills

**M**aintaining and troubleshooting technology can involve several abilities, including setting up routines for maintenance, working with mechanical devices, and using logic to pinpoint the cause of a problem. Look for opportunities to develop this skill in school and your extracurricular activities.

### Education

- Study science to learn how to apply logical thinking to technical problems.
- Take courses that teach you about computer hardware and operating systems.
- Take shop, electronics, or other technical courses to learn how machines work.

### Activities

- Find a machine in your house and read the manual to see how it should be maintained. Does your family do a good job of maintaining it?
- If you like to work with computers, offer to help older relatives or neighbors who may be unsure how to maintain their computers or fix minor problems.
- Consider what would happen if an important piece of technology, such as the family car or the computers at the stock exchange, broke down. What would happen?

# Try It Yourself

**Y**ou work for a medium-sized accounting company as the office manager. One day in the middle of your busy tax season, the copier breaks down. How would you handle the situation? Here are some tips:

1. Use the manual and instructions on the machine to see whether you can figure out the problem. See whether there is a troubleshooting section you can refer to.

2. Check to make sure that somebody has performed all the routine maintenance functions. If something has been missed, would taking care of it now solve the problem?

3. If the problem is serious or you can't figure it out, call the service company for the copier. Always keep service phone numbers and policy numbers handy!

4. If the machine is new and under warranty, you may have to contact the company that sold it to you to fix it.

To keep the machines you work with running smoothly, keep these guidelines in mind:

- Give the machine what it needs to run. Depending on the machine, this might involve oiling some working parts, running a virus scan on a computer, or keeping the ink supply full, for example.

- Repair small problems before they become big ones. If you notice a small problem, such as unusual lines running through all your copies or frequent computer crashes, try to find and fix the problem before it becomes worse.

- Perform maintenance routinely. Set a schedule to do routine maintenance and stick to it.

# Performance Review

**W**hat rating would an employer give you on maintaining and troubleshooting technology?

- Needs Improvement
- Average
- Above Average
- Outstanding

Take action to earn an Outstanding rating by consistently doing the tasks in the following checklist.

---

## MAINTAINING AND TROUBLESHOOTING TECHNOLOGY CHECKLIST

○ Read any manuals that come with the technology. These provide good advice on maintenance schedules and troubleshooting.

○ Examine the machine to see whether you can figure out the problem. This often involves a process of eliminating possibilities one by one.

○ Know how to contact the people who can help you fix problems with the technology.

---

# Words at Work

**T**hese words relate to maintaining and troubleshooting technology. How many can you define?

- Troubleshoot
- Bug
- Malfunction
- Equipment
- Service
- Repair

# MORE CAREER SKILLS RESOURCES

**P**reparing for the career of your choice is an important task. The following useful and informative resources are a good starting point for career exploration.

## Web Sites and Other Online Resources

- About.com is a huge informational site that includes various articles on career planning and even a free career planning online course. **www.careerplanning.about.com**

- Careers.org is a career site that's jam-packed with more than 1,000 pages of career building information. **www.careers.org**

- Go to the Firstgov for Kids site and click the Careers link to get links to helpful sites and publications on career skills. **www.kids.gov/**

- The Get Career Skills site is managed by the Association for Career and Technical Education (ACTE), which is a national educational organization. This site provides a variety of career-related information and links. **www.getcareerskills.com**

- GetTech is a great site for exploring a wide variety of technical careers. **www.gettech.org**

- Visit the JIST Publishing site (publishers of this book) to check out the free career resources such as the JIST Tips and Best Jobs Lists. **www.jist.com**

- The Mindtools site offers a free e-newsletter on career skills as well as free information on several key job skills. **www.mindtools.com**

- Skills USA is a nonprofit organization that works with students and teachers to help develop career skills. They sponsor competitions in demonstrating career skills for students as well as career development workshops. **www.skillsusa.org**

- This link at the U.S. Department of Labor Web site takes you to the original SCANS report (the career skills list this book is based on). **http://wdr.doleta.gov/SCANS/whatwork/**

# Books and Other Materials

- *Young Person's Character Education Handbook.* Several career skills, such as being honest and leading, are considered character traits. This book is designed to help you understand these and other important character traits so that you can make good choices and do the right thing. It includes examples from school subjects, checklists, case studies, and vocabulary lists for each trait.

- *Young Person's Occupational Outlook Handbook.* To find more careers that interest you, check out this book. Based on the Department of Labor's *Occupational Outlook Handbook,* this book describes about 270 jobs. Each description includes information about related school subjects, required training, earnings, and employment outlook. Related jobs are grouped together to make it easy for you to explore jobs that match your interests.

- *Dream Catchers.* This workbook uses stories and activities to start you thinking about the skills you have and how they match up with different careers.

- *Career & Life Explorer.* This assessment connects your interests, hobbies, favorite school subjects, and more to possible career options. Part of the assessment is a "My Ideal Job" poster to hang in your locker or room.

- *Exploring Your Career Options.* This video shows you how to go about finding information on careers that interest you. In the video, students describe what they like to do and use that information to figure out what careers to explore. The video is packed with ideas you can use to find a career that's right for you.

- *Career Connections Jr. CD-ROM.* Connect your interests to careers by playing games such as Career Pursuit and 20 Questions. This software also includes photos and information for more than 260 jobs.

The books, video, and software may be in your school or public library. All products are available at www.jist.com or by calling 1-800-648-JIST.

# CORE SUBJECTS AND YOUR CAREER

**S**tudents often wonder why they must study subjects that seem unrelated to their career goals. Why does a future engineer need to take English classes? How does math help an air traffic controller direct planes? When do chefs or cooks use science and technology in the kitchen?

This appendix explains the importance of English, math, and science in your career preparation. For students with an interest or aptitude in a subject, the sections explain the link between that subject and a number of careers. Each section also describes how we use English, math, and science in everyday life and lists occupations requiring various levels of competence.

Of course, you should consult detailed references, such as the *Occupational Outlook Handbook*, in making career decisions. But this appendix may serve as a reminder that a good foundation is essential for success.

# English and Your Career

Reading and writing are basic skills we begin learning at a young age. So why do we need to continue studying them in high school and beyond? Taking English classes improves communication skills, which are essential to every job.

Communication is the ability to understand information other people give us and to have other people understand what we tell them. In addition to being fundamental for most jobs, the ability to communicate clearly and effectively can help us in every area of our lives. Every time we write a letter, make a phone call, or give someone instructions, we use communication skills. Studying English helps us develop our reading, writing, speaking, and listening skills, all of which play some part in our everyday lives.

## Taking English in High School and College

In high school English classes, most students study basics such as vocabulary, spelling, composition, reading, and grammar. Learning how to construct sentences and paragraphs lays the groundwork for writing effective letters, essays, term papers, and reports. English classes also include exposure to literature, which teaches students to analyze other people's words and provokes thought by providing insight into the human condition.

College-level English courses are designed to refine the skills learned in high school. Subjects such as literature, writing, and grammar are taught as individual classes. These courses provide additional study and practice of communication.

## How English Relates to Careers

You may think English classes only relate to a few occupations, such as writing or editing. But every job requires workers to understand instructions quickly and to explain problems to supervisors and other workers.

Good communication is essential for most occupations, even those that require little interaction with others. A problem cited by employers of engineers, for example, is that some technically competent workers are unable to explain what they are doing, to understand or explain what their part of a project is, or to relate their task to what others are doing.

## Jobs Requiring Basic Communication Skills

Basic communication requires the ability to interact with others and to follow simple oral and written instructions; high school English classes are helpful but not essential in developing this level of skill.

The following jobs require basic communication skills:

Bank tellers

Bus drivers

Cashiers

Correctional officers

Counter and rental clerks

Court reporters, medical transcriptionists, and stenographers

Dispatchers

Flight attendants

Funeral directors

General office clerks

Homemaker—home health aides

Hotel and motel desk clerks

Interviewing and new accounts clerks

Loan clerks and credit authorizers, checkers, and clerks

Nursing aides and psychiatric aides

Occupational therapy assistants and aides

Physical and corrective therapy assistants and aides

Postal clerks and mail carriers

Prepress workers

Preschool teachers and child care workers

Proofreaders

Receptionists

Reservation and transportation ticket agents and travel clerks

Routing and receiving clerks

Service representatives

Taxi drivers and chauffeurs

Telephone operators

Title searchers

Typesetters

Typists, word processors, and data entry keyers

Visual artists

Many occupations require frequent communication. Sales workers must be able to speak effectively both on the telephone and in person to present their company's products well. Lawyers and managers need to express themselves clearly and analyze large amounts of information to be successful. Health care workers must be able to understand their patients' questions and concerns and help patients understand how to maintain their health. Psychologists and psychiatrists must be able to listen and communicate effectively.

## Developing Communication Skills

The best way to begin developing communication skills is to take high school English classes. Reading outside of class is also a good way to develop those skills and build an effective vocabulary. In addition, getting involved in extracurricular activities improves communication because of the interaction required. Some activities target specific abilities: Joining the school newspaper or yearbook staff is a good way to work on writing skills; the debate team is ideal for developing speaking skills.

## Jobs Requiring Intermediate Communication Skills

Intermediate communication requires the ability to accurately give and follow instructions, to persuade people to a particular point of view, and to write in an organized and grammatically correct manner; both high school and college English courses are helpful in developing these skills.

The following jobs require intermediate communication skills:

Adjusters, investigators, and collectors

Architects

Clerical supervisors and managers

Construction and building inspectors

Construction and building managers

Designers

Employment interviewers

Financial managers

Health information technicians

Health services managers

Hotel managers and assistants

Industrial production managers

Insurance agents and brokers

Library technicians

Licensed practical nurses

Paralegals

Pharmacists

Physical therapists

Police, detectives, and special agents

Private detectives and investigators

Property managers

Real estate agents, brokers, and appraisers

Receptionists

Recreation workers

Recreational therapists

Registered nurses

Respiratory therapists

Restaurant and food service managers

Retail sales worker supervisors and managers

Retail sales workers

Secretaries

Securities and financial services sales representatives

Service sales representatives

Social and human service assistants

Travel agents

Travel guides

## Jobs Requiring Advanced Communication Skills

Advanced communication requires a strong ability to communicate both orally and in writing; college-level English courses are recommended.

The following jobs require advanced communication skills:

Actors, directors, and producers

Administrative services managers

Adult education teachers

Agricultural scientists

Biological and medical scientists

Chemists

Engineering, science, and computer systems managers

Foresters and conservation scientists

Geologists and geophysicists

Government chief executives and legislators

Lawyers and judges

Librarians

Management analysts and consultants

Manufacturers' and wholesale sales representatives

Marketing, advertising, and public relations managers

Meteorologists

Optometrists

Pharmacists

Physician assistants

Physicians

Physicists and astronomers

Podiatrists

Psychologists

Public relations specialists

Radio and television announcers and newscasters

Reporters and correspondents

School teachers, kindergarten, elementary, and secondary

*continued*

*continued*

| | |
|---|---|
| **Social scientists** | **Urban and regional planners** |
| **Social workers** | **Veterinarians** |
| **Special education teachers** | **Writers and editors** |
| **Speech-language pathologists and audiologists** | |

The accompanying lists show occupations that require advanced, intermediate, or basic communication skills. Advanced communication requires a strong ability to communicate both orally and in writing; college-level English courses are recommended. Intermediate communication requires the ability to accurately give and follow instructions, to persuade people to a particular point of view, and to write in an organized and grammatically correct manner; both high school and college English courses are helpful in developing these skills. Basic communication requires the ability to interact with others and to follow simple oral and written instructions; high school English classes are helpful but not essential in developing this level of skill.

# Math and Your Career

Math skills help us cope with today's complex world. We use math to carry out everyday tasks such as balancing a checkbook, shopping for groceries, cooking, and creating a personal budget. Other important skills we learn from studying math include problem solving, analysis, and estimating. And math knowledge is essential for earning a living in many occupations, including most higher-paying occupations.

About 15,500 mathematicians are employed in the United States, but millions of workers have jobs in which mathematics is a necessary part. In fact, almost all jobs require at least some understanding of basic mathematics. For example, carpenters must be able to measure lengths and angles when installing wood trim. Machinists need to understand and manipulate angles and dimensions. Loan officers must determine applicants' debt-equity ratios before approving mortgage applications. And math skills are required for any science, engineering, computer, and technical occupation.

Math is also an important part of a well-rounded education. Most high schools require students to take at least two years of math to graduate. And most colleges require some proficiency in math for all applicants, regardless of their intended majors.

## Careers for People Interested in Math

Although most occupations require basic math skills, some jobs rely on math more heavily than others. If you have taken many math courses, have a high aptitude for math, or major in math in college, you might be interested in some of the following occupations.

*Actuaries.* Actuaries answer questions about future risk, formulate investment strategies, and make pricing decisions. They may design insurance, financial, and pension plans by calculating probabilities of events such as sickness, disability, or death based on known statistics.

A bachelor's degree in mathematics or statistics is required for an entry-level position in a life or casualty insurance company. Applicants must be proficient in several mathematics subjects, including calculus, probability, and statistics, and have passed the beginning actuarial exams.

*Mathematicians.* Mathematicians use their mathematical knowledge and computational tools to create mathematical theories and techniques. They use these theories and techniques to solve economic, scientific, engineering, and business problems. Mathematicians often work with computers to solve problems, develop models, analyze relationships between variables, and process large amounts of data.

Mathematicians need a minimum of a bachelor's degree. People with bachelor's degrees may assist senior mathematicians or work on less advanced problems. Most mathematicians in the private sector need a master's or doctoral degree.

*Operations research analysts.* Operations research analysts are problem solvers who usually work for large organizations or businesses. They help these organizations operate more efficiently by applying mathematics principles to organizational issues. They work on problems such as facilities layout, personnel schedules, forecasting, and distribution systems. They often use mathematical models to explain how things happen within an organization and to determine how to organize things more effectively.

Most employers prefer to hire analysts who have a master's degree in operations research, industrial engineering, or management science.

*Statisticians.* Statisticians collect, analyze, and present numerical data. They also design, carry out, and interpret the results of surveys and experiments. Statisticians use mathematics techniques to predict things such as economic conditions or population growth, to develop quality control tests for manufactured products, and to help business managers or government officials make decisions and evaluate the results of new programs.

For most beginning jobs in statistics, a bachelor's degree in mathematics or statistics is the minimum requirement. Many research positions require a master's or doctoral degree.

# Jobs Requiring General Mathematics Skills

Occupations in the general math skills category require basic arithmetic such as addition, subtraction, multiplication, and division.

The following jobs require general mathematics skills:

Bank tellers

Billing clerks and billing machine operators

Bindery workers

Bookkeeping, accounting, and auditing clerks

Bricklayers and stonemasons

Brokerage clerks and statement clerks

Cashiers

Counter and rental clerks

Drywall workers and lathers

Glaziers

Interviewing and new accounts clerks

Library assistants and bookmobile drivers

Loan clerks and credit authorizers, checkers, and clerks

Manufacturers' and wholesale sales representatives

Medical assistants

Metalworking and plastic-working machine operators

Order clerks

Payroll and timekeeping clerks

Plasterers

Postal clerks and mail carriers

Precision assemblers

Prepress workers

Printing press operators

Private detectives and investigators

Reservation and transportation ticket agents and travel clerks

Roofers

Secretaries

Stock clerks

Structural and reinforcing iron-workers

Taxi drivers and chauffeurs

Teacher aides

Tilesetters

Traffic, shipping, and receiving clerks

# Careers Requiring Strong Math Skills

Some other jobs require a strong background in math. The following occupations are among those in which strong math skills are very important.

*Physical and life scientists.* Physical and life scientists, including biologists, physicists, chemists, and geologists, work to discover the basic principles of how the earth, universe, and living things operate. The ability to use mathematical relationships to understand and describe the workings of nature is vital.

Most scientists need a doctoral degree in their field, especially those who work in basic research, but some scientists in applied research may need only a bachelor's or master's degree.

# Jobs Requiring Practical Application of Mathematics

Occupations in the practical math category may require algebra and geometry in addition to general math skills.

The following jobs require the practical application of mathematics skills:

Air traffic controllers

Aircraft mechanics, including engine specialists

Automobile mechanics

Automotive body repairers

Blue-collar worker supervisors

Boilermakers

Broadcast technicians

Carpenters

Concrete masons and terrazzo workers

Diesel mechanics

*continued*

*continued*

| | |
|---|---|
| Dietitians and nutritionists | Machinists and tool programmers |
| Electric power generating plant operators and power distributors and dispatchers | Millwrights |
| | Mobile heavy equipment mechanics |
| Electricians | Motorcycle, boat, and small-engine repairers |
| Electronic equipment repairers | |
| Elevator installers and repairers | Ophthalmic laboratory technicians |
| Farm equipment mechanics | Photographers and camera operators |
| Funeral directors | |
| General maintenance mechanics | Purchasers and buyers |
| Heating, air-conditioning, and refrigeration technicians | Sheet metal workers |
| | Stationary engineers |
| Industrial machinery repairers | Tool-and-die makers |
| Inspectors, testers, and graders | Water and wastewater treatment plant operators |
| Jewelers | |
| Landscape architects | Welders, cutters, and welding machine operators |

*Social scientists.* Social scientists perform research that helps us understand how individuals and groups make decisions, exercise power, and respond to change. Many social scientists, especially economists, describe behavior with mathematical models. Also, much of social scientists' research depends on gathering and understanding statistics that describe human behavior.

As with physical and life scientists, many jobs involving research require a doctorate. However, many social science jobs involving applied research require only a bachelor's or master's degree.

*Computer scientists and systems analysts.* Workers in computer science occupations design computer systems and perform research to improve these systems. They may also program computers. Advanced mathematics skills might not be necessary for computer programming; however, training in mathematics helps develop an ability to think logically—a necessary qualification for working with computers.

Most of these workers have bachelor's degrees in computer science, information systems, or computer engineering. Some research positions require a master's or doctoral degree.

*Engineers.* Engineers use the theories and principles of mathematics to help solve technical problems. They also use mathematics to design machinery, products, or systems. Most entry-level engineering jobs require a bachelor's degree.

*Science and engineering technicians.* Science and engineering technicians use the principles and theories of science, engineering, and mathematics to solve technical problems in research and development, manufacturing, and other areas. Their jobs are more limited in scope and more practically oriented than those of scientists and engineers, but technicians rely heavily on mathematics techniques in their work.

There are many different ways of qualifying for a position as a science and engineering technician, but most jobs require at least some training beyond earning a high school diploma.

## Jobs Requiring Applied Mathematics Skills

Occupations in the applied math skills category include those in which workers need to understand mathematical concepts and be able to apply them to their work; in these occupations, knowledge of statistics and trigonometry may also be needed.

The following jobs require applied mathematics skills:

**Accountants and auditors**

**Administrative services managers**

**Aircraft pilots**

**Budget analysts**

**Chiropractors**

**College and university faculty (nonmathematics)**

**Computer programmers**

**Construction and building inspectors**

**Construction contractors and managers**

**Cost estimators**

**Dentists**

**Dispensing opticians**

**Drafters**

**Education administrators**

**Engineering technicians**

**Farmers and farm managers**

**Financial managers**

*continued*

*continued*

General managers and top executives

Government chief executives and legislators

Industrial production managers

Insurance agents and brokers

Insurance underwriters

Loan officers and counselors

Management analysts and consultants

Optometrists

Pharmacists

Physician assistants

Physicians

Podiatrists

Psychologists

Real estate agents, brokers, and appraisers

Respiratory therapists

School teachers, kindergarten, elementary, and secondary

Science technicians

Securities and financial services sales representatives

Special education teachers

Surveyors and mapping scientists

Urban and regional planners

Veterinarians

# Other Careers that Require Math Skills

Math skills are useful in a number of other occupations. For example, most jobs in the financial industry use math skills. Bank tellers must have strong math skills to be both accurate and efficient. Accountants need proficiency in math to calculate and analyze numbers. Air traffic controllers need to understand maps and geometry when directing planes. Managers of all kinds use math skills; for example, hotel managers and assistants must be able to estimate costs for items the hotel needs to order, such as food and drinks.

# Preparing for Careers in Math

The accompanying lists show occupations that require different levels of math skills: advanced, applied, practical, or general. Occupations in the advanced or theoretical math skills category require an understanding of more complex math concepts such as calculus and linear algebra. Occupations in the applied math skills category include those in which workers need to understand mathematical concepts and be able to apply them to their work; in these occupations, knowledge of statistics and trigonometry may also be needed. Occupations in the practical math category may require algebra and geometry in addition to general math skills. Occupations in the general math skills category require basic arithmetic such as addition, subtraction, multiplication, and division.

## Jobs Requiring Advanced or Theoretical Mathematics Skills

Occupations in the advanced or theoretical math skills category require an understanding of more complex math concepts such as calculus and linear algebra.

The following jobs require advanced or theoretical mathematics skills:

Actuaries

Agricultural scientists

Architects

Biological and medical scientists

Chemists

Computer scientists, computer engineers, and systems analysts

Economists and marketing research analysts

Engineering, science, and data-processing managers

Engineers

Foresters and conservation scientists

Geologists, geophysicists, and oceanographers

Mathematicians

Mathematics teachers (secondary school and college)

Meteorologists

Operations research analysts

Physicists and astronomers

Social scientists

Statisticians

# Science and Your Career

Studying science helps us understand the discoveries that affect our daily lives. Every time we use a telephone, television, or computer, we are using a product of science. We use our knowledge of science when making decisions about our health and diet. Even common hobbies, such as cooking, gardening, and photography, rely on scientific principles.

By studying science, we learn how the universe works; we learn to observe, classify, measure, predict, interpret, and communicate data; and we develop the ability to think logically and solve problems. The skills and knowledge that come from studying science are important in many occupations.

Almost 400,000 scientists are employed in the United States, but 21 million workers use science on the job. For example, mechanics use scientific procedures when repairing or testing equipment. Physical therapists use biology and physics to rehabilitate patients. Journalists use scientific knowledge when writing about technology, health, or the environment. And scientific problem-solving skills are necessary for most computer occupations.

Science courses are also important if you want an advanced education. College admissions officers often favor individuals who have taken science classes. Many colleges require at least two years of high school science courses, regardless of your intended major. If you want to be admitted into scientific and technical programs, you will probably need three or four years of high school science.

## *Careers for People Interested in Science*

Although science skills are helpful in many occupations, some occupations rely heavily on science. If you have a strong interest in science, you might want to consider one of the following occupations.

*Biologists.* Biologists study living organisms and their relationship to each other and the environment. Most biologists specialize in one branch of biology—for example, microbiology, the study of microscopic organisms; zoology, the study of animals; or botany, the study of plants. These branches are then subdivided. For example, types of zoologists include mammalogists, who study mammals; ichthyologists, who study fish; ornithologists, who study birds; and herpetologists, who study reptiles and amphibians.

Young Person's Career Skills Handbook, © JIST Works

# Jobs Requiring the Practical Application of Science Skills

Practical application occupations require familiarity with the basic principles of biology, chemistry, or physics; high school courses in these areas should be sufficient.

The following jobs require the practical application of science skills:

Automotive body repairers

Automotive mechanics

Barbers and cosmetologists

Boilermakers

Chefs, cooks, and other kitchen workers

Dental assistants

Diesel mechanics

Electricians

Electronic equipment repairers

Elevator installers and repairers

Farm equipment mechanics

Farmers and farm managers

Firefighting occupations

Fishers, hunters, and trappers

Funeral directors

General maintenance mechanics

Heating, air-conditioning, and refrigeration technicians

Home appliance and power tool repairers

Industrial machinery repairers

Jewelers

Landscaping, groundskeeping, nursery, greenhouse, and lawn service occupations

Machinists and tool programmers

Medical assistants

Millwrights

Mobile heavy equipment mechanics

Motorcycle, boat, and small-engine mechanics

Nursing aides and psychiatric aides

Ophthalmic laboratory technicians

Pest controllers

Pharmacy technicians

Photographic process workers

Physical and corrective therapy assistants

Plumbers and pipefitters

Prepress workers

Printing press operators

Stationary engineers

Structural and reinforcing iron workers

Tool-and-die makers

Urban and regional planners

Vending machine servicers and repairers

Water and wastewater treatment plant operators

Water transportation occupations

Welders, cutters, and welding machine operators

*Chemists.* Chemists search for new chemicals and find uses for existing ones. Their discoveries might be used to produce medicines or create stronger building materials. Some chemists specialize in one branch of chemistry. Biochemists, for example, study the chemical composition of living things. Physical chemists examine the physical characteristics of atoms, molecules, and chemical reactions.

*Physicists.* Physicists study the behavior of matter, the generation and transfer of energy, and the interaction of matter and energy. They study areas such as gravity, nuclear energy, electromagnetism, electricity, light, and heat. They might examine the structure of the atom or design research equipment such as lasers. Physicists might also work in inspection, testing, or other production-related jobs.

*Agricultural scientists.* Some types of scientists work to improve agriculture. Crop scientists study the genetic breeding and management of field crops. Soil scientists use soil physics, soil chemistry, and soil microbiology to enhance soil fertility and the growth of plants. Agronomists develop practical applications for discoveries in plant and soil science to produce high-quality food.

*Other scientists.* There are many other branches of science. Geologists study the history and composition of our planet, including volcanoes and earthquakes. Oceanographers study the oceans and their movements. Meteorologists study the atmosphere, and some make weather predictions. Astronomers study the universe, trying to gain knowledge about the stars, planets, and galaxies.

## Jobs Requiring Applied Science Skills

Applied science occupations require workers to understand scientific principles and apply them to their work; some post-high school science training is needed. The following jobs require applied science skills:

Aircraft mechanics, including engine specialists

Aircraft pilots

Broadcast technicians

Cardiovascular technologists and technicians

Clinical laboratory technologists and technicians

College and university faculty

Construction and building inspectors

Construction contractors and managers

| | |
|---|---|
| Dental hygienists | Occupational therapists |
| Dental laboratory technicians | Occupational therapy assistants and aides |
| Dietitians and nutritionists | |
| Dispensing opticians | Photographers and camera operators |
| Drafters | |
| Electroneurodiagnostic technologists | Physical therapists |
| | Psychologists |
| Electronic semiconductor processors | Radiologic technologists |
| | Recreational therapists |
| Emergency medical technicians | Registered nurses |
| Engineering technicians (all specialties) | Respiratory therapists |
| | Science technicians |
| Health information technicians | Speech-language pathologists and audiologists |
| Health services managers | |
| Licensed practical nurses | Surgical technologists |
| Nuclear medicine technologists | Surveyors and mapping scientists |

Although many scientists specialize, most need to have knowledge in more than one branch of science. Agronomists, for example, combine their knowledge of biology, geology, chemistry, and mathematics to find better ways to grow food and conserve soil. They may also work closely with other scientists, such as micro-biologists, biochemists, meteorologists, and entomologists.

*Engineers.* Engineers use the principles and theories of chemistry, physics, and mathematics to solve practical problems. They develop new products and improve systems and processes. Engineers design computers, generators, helicopters, spacecraft, and other devices. Engineering has many specialties. The largest are mechanical engineering, electrical and electronics engineering, and civil engineering.

Mechanical engineers design and develop power-producing machines, such as internal combustion and rocket engines. Others design and develop power-using machines, such as refrigeration systems.

Electrical and electronics engineers design, develop, test, and supervise the production of electrical equipment. This includes computers, automobile ignition systems, and wiring and lighting in buildings. They also design communications, video, and radar equipment.

Civil engineers design and supervise the building of roads, bridges, tunnels, buildings, airports, harbors, and water supply, flood control, and sewage systems.

## Jobs Requiring Advanced Science Skills

Advanced science occupations require a thorough knowledge of scientific principles; a bachelor's degree with a number of college science courses is usually the minimum requirement. But many of these positions require a master's or doctoral degree.

The following jobs require advanced science skills:

| | |
|---|---|
| **Agricultural scientists** | **Geologists and geophysicists** |
| **Architects** | **Landscape architects** |
| **Archivists and curators** | **Meteorologists** |
| **Biological and medical scientists** | **Optometrists** |
| **Chemists** | **Pharmacists** |
| **Chiropractors** | **Physical therapists** |
| **Computer scientists, computer engineers, and systems analysts** | **Physician assistants** |
| **Dentists** | **Physicians** |
| **Engineering, science, and computer systems managers** | **Physicists and astronomers** |
| **Engineers** | **Podiatrists** |
| **Forensic scientists** | **Respiratory therapists** |
| **Foresters and conservation scientists** | **Teachers, secondary and college (sciences)** |
| | **Veterinarians** |

*Technicians and technologists.* Science and engineering technicians carry out the plans of scientists and engineers—setting up experiments, recording results, or testing product quality. They may also design simple experiments. These workers use testing and measuring devices and have a solid understanding of laboratory techniques.

Other technician occupations include drafters, who prepare technical drawings of structures and products; broadcast technicians, who install, repair, and operate radio and television equipment; and air-conditioning, refrigeration, and heating technicians.

## Other Careers that Use Science

Science skills are useful in many other occupations. For example, there are numerous occupations in health care, and all require knowledge of biology and other sciences. Physicians, nurses, dentists, veterinarians, and emergency medical technicians are just a few of the health occupations that require an understanding of science.

Many workers use chemistry and physics in their work. Chefs and cooks use chemistry when creating recipes and preparing food, because cooking ingredients are chemicals. Dietitians and nutritionists are also concerned with chemical content of foods. Farmers and horticulturists use fertilizers and pesticides, the products of chemistry. Electricians apply the principles of physics when wiring a building, and aircraft pilots use physics and meteorology to plot flight paths and fly planes.

## Preparing for Careers in Science

Careers in science require orderly thinking, systematic work habits, and perseverance. If you are a student who is interested in scientific and technical careers, you should take as many science classes in high school as possible. Basic courses in earth science, biology, chemistry, and physics will form a solid foundation for further study. A strong background in mathematics is also important for those who want to pursue scientific, engineering, and technology-related careers.

The lists show occupations requiring different levels of scientific skill: advanced, applied, or practical application. Advanced science occupations require a thorough knowledge of scientific principles; a bachelor's degree with a number of college science courses is usually the minimum requirement. Many of these positions require a master's or doctoral degree. Applied science occupations require workers to understand scientific principles and apply them to their work; some post-high school science training is needed. Practical application occupations require familiarity with the basic principles of biology, chemistry, or physics; high school courses in these areas should be sufficient.

Appendix B is from the *Occupational Outlook Quarterly* by the U.S. Department of Labor. Written by Nancy Saffer, an economist formerly with the Office of Employment Projections, BLS.